A garden is a grand teacher.
It teaches patience
and careful watchfulness;
it teaches industry and thrift;
above all it teaches entire trust.

— Gertrude Jekyll

THE Garden Tourist

*120 Destination Gardens
and Nurseries in the Northeast*

JANA MILBOCKER

Enchanted Gardens

Cover: Chanticleer Garden, Wayne, PA
Above: Blithewold, Bristol, RI

Copyright ©2018 by Jana Milbocker

Published by Enchanted Gardens
For ordering information please contact
Enchanted Gardens, P.O. Box 6433, Holliston, MA 01746, 508-494-8768, thegardentourist@gmail.com

Cover and interior designed by Jana Milbocker. Photo credits appear on page 254.
Edited by Charlotte Bruce Harvey
Printed in China

Publisher's Cataloging-in-Publication Data
provided by Five Rainbows Cataloging Services
Milbocker, Jana.
The garden tourist : 120 destination gardens and nurseries in the northeast / Jana Milbocker.
Holliston, MA : Enchanted Gardens, 2018.
ISBN 978-0-9988335-0-7 (pbk.)
LCSH: Garden tours. | Gardens, American--Pictorial works. | Northeastern States--Guidebooks. | Travel--Guidebooks. | Illustrated works. | BISAC: TRAVEL / United States / Northeast / General.
LCC SB457.53 .M55 2018 (print) | LCC SB457.53 (ebook) | DDC 635.022/2--dc23.
Library of Congress Control Number: 2017915051

First Edition

THE
Garden
Tourist

*120 Destination Gardens and
Nurseries in the Northeast*

Garden Index

How to use this book

This guide is for travelers who wish to visit some of the most enchanting gardens and nurseries in the Northeast, from northern New England to the Hudson River Valley, New Jersey, and eastern Pennsylvania.

The book is divided into seven chapters covering the major states. Each chapter features a state map with a list of the gardens, as well as suggested itineraries for making the best of your visit. Each garden entry includes the address, telephone, and website; the size of the garden, visiting hours, special events, and facilities.

AMENITIES KEY

 House tour available

 Restrooms

 Shop

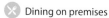 Dining on premises

Children's garden or programming

Please call or refer to each garden's website to confirm opening times and activities. Many of the gardens and nurseries have different operating hours depending on the season.

The admission fees listed in the book are current at the time of publication, and indicate regular adult admission. Discounts for seniors, children, and students may be available.

On the itineraries page are suggested restaurants for lunch or tea. These are mid-priced venues with a menu that accommodates a range of tastes, and were chosen solely by the author.

Get Inspired!

Twenty-five years ago I moved into a century-old house, and that first spring I held my breath each morning as I walked around the yard, scanning the soil to see what would pop out of it. I imagined generations of gardeners leaving a horticultural blueprint for me to follow, but as spring turned to summer and no bulbs or peony nubs had emerged, I saw that I had more or less a blank slate: almost two acres populated with old trees, overgrown shrubs, and large lawns. With mixed feelings (panic, excitement!) I turned to books and classes for education and inspiration, and I soon found that by visiting other gardens I could observe and learn about new plant varieties and advantageous plant combinations, as well as garden design techniques and cultural practices.

My thirst for gardening knowledge has only increased since then. I annually visit about 15 gardens—on organized garden tours, vacations, business trips, and even college campus tours. I enjoy returning to many of the same gardens and estates year after year. Observing a landscape during different seasons and weather conditions—even at different times of day—yields valuable lessons that I can take home to my own garden.

And I have found I am not alone! Friends and relatives—even non-gardeners—who've accompanied me on my garden jaunts enthusiastically volunteer to come again. This seems to be part of a growing trend throughout the United States and worldwide. Central Connecticut State University professor Richard W. Benfield, author of *Garden Tourism*, estimates that 100 million people visited U.S. public gardens in 2016—more than Las Vegas and Orlando combined. They visited gardens to be outdoors, to enjoy beauty, to relieve stress, and to enjoy being with others.

The Northeast is seeing an exciting resurgence in garden creation and restoration. The Coastal Maine Botanical Gardens is the brainchild of lo-

cals who believed northern New England needed a botanical garden. Grand Massachusetts estates such as Edith Wharton's The Mount, The Crane Estate, and Naumkeag recently have been restored to their Gilded Age glory with the generous and enthusiastic support of private donors. The Garden Conservancy has been invaluable in preserving private gardens for public enjoyment, and a growing number of important landscapes have been designated as National Historic Landmarks. There is a growing realization that gardens matter.

This book is a virtual garden tour of large public gardens, historic estates, inspiring private gardens, and destination nurseries from Maine through New England to New York's Hudson River Valley, eastern Pennsylvania, and New Jersey. It's not an exhaustive list, but a selection to illustrated the horticultural richness of the Northeast. I particularly enjoy discovering small home nurseries born of a gardener's initial fascination with a particular plant, and I find that visiting historic homes with preserved gardens gives me a sense of stepping back in time. Gardens that incorporate art, sculp-

ture, or music demonstrate the imagination and possibilities that can define the holistic horticultural experience.

Gardens truly are reflections of their creators. Many large public gardens such as Longwood Gardens and the New York Botanical Garden were initially born of their founder's passion for plants. Talk with the current owners and caretakers and learn something new. This guide includes an introduction to some of the extraordinary individuals who took their passion for horticulture and created a retreat that others can enjoy for years to come.

While many of these gardens were built by wealthy landowners, they owe their continued existence to volunteers. Few estates can now afford the staff required to maintain these landscapes, relying on a small army of volunteers, many of whom have given their hard work and knowledge for more than 30 years. It is with gratitude and appreciation that I visit these special places. I hope to inspire you to experience many of these beautiful destinations on your own.

Grounds for Sculpture

Vermont, New Hampshire, Maine

SUGGESTED DAILY ITINERARIES

VERMONT
Morning
Hildene, Manchester (1)
Lunch–The Perfect Wife, Manchester
Walker Farm, East Dummerston (2)

NEW HAMPSHIRE/VERMONT
Morning
Tarbin Garden, Franklin (5)
The Fells, Newbury
Lunch–Bubba's Bar & Grille, Newbury
Saint Gaudens Historic Site, Cornish (4)
Cider Hill Gardens & Gallery, Windsor VT (3)

NEW HAMPSHIRE
Morning
Fuller Gardens, North Hampton (13)
Lunch–Seacoast Soups, North Hampton
Bedrock Gardens, Lee (7)

APPLEDORE ISLAND
All Day
Celia Thaxter's Garden, Appledore Island (8)

NEW HAMPSHIRE
Morning
Rundlet-May House, Portsmouth (9)
Moffatt-Ladd House, Portsmouth (10)
Lunch–The River House, Portsmouth
Prescott Park, Portsmouth (11)
Strawberry Banke, Portsmouth (12)

NEW HAMPSHIRE
Mason Hollow Nursery, Mason (14)
Lunch–Pickity Place (15)

MAINE
Morning
Hamilton House, South Berwick (16)
Snug Harbor Farm, Kennebunk (17)
Lunch–Red's Eats, Wiscasset
Nickels-Sortwell House, Wiscasset (18)

MAINE
Morning
Coastal Maine Botanical Gardens, Boothbay (19)
Lunch–Coastal Maine Botanical café
Boat ride or kayaking at Coastal Maine

13 **14** **19**

Vermont, New Hampshire, Maine

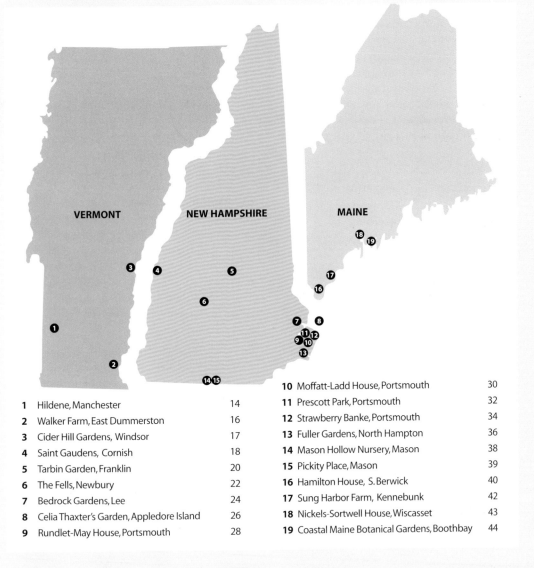

VERMONT

NEW HAMPSHIRE

MAINE

Hildene

1005 Hildene Rd., Manchester, VT 05254
(800) 578-1788
hildene.org

AREA: 400 acres

HOURS: Daily 9:30–4:30

ADMISSION: $20 includes home, garden, entire estate

AMENITIES:

EVENTS: Lectures, Celebration of Peonies mid-May to mid-June

Hildene was the estate of Robert Todd Lincoln, the only child of Abraham and Mary Todd Lincoln to survive to adulthood. It remained the family home of Lincoln descendants until 1975, when Mary Lincoln Beckwith, Robert's granddaughter, died there. Threatened by the prospect of a sale to private developers, neighbors and community members fought for three years to save Hildene. In 1978, the Friends of Hildene purchased the property and began restoration of the house, outbuildings, and gardens.

Born in 1843, Robert Todd Lincoln became chairman of the Pullman Palace Car Company, the largest manufacturing corporation at the turn

of the 20th century. In addition to his career as a lawyer and CEO, Lincoln served as Secretary of War from 1881 to 1885 under Presidents Garfield and Arthur, and U.S. Ambassador to the United Kingdom from 1889 to 1893 under President Harrison. Lincoln built Hildene as a summer home for his family, taking the name Hildene from the Old English words meaning "hill and valley with stream." Completed in 1905 in the Georgian Revival style, the house stands on a 300-foot promontory overlooking the Battenkill Valley with stunning views in all directions. Hildene is furnished almost entirely with Lincoln family furniture, and contains artifacts belonging to Robert Todd Lincoln and his parents. Of special interest is the foyer's 1,000-pipe Aeolian organ, which is played during house tours.

Frederick Todd, an apprentice of Frederick Law Olmstead, designed Hildene's grounds, with the exception of a formal garden on the south lawn, which Lincoln's daughter, Jessie, created as a gift for her mother. Jessie's design was influenced by French parterres she had seen while the family lived in Europe. When seen from her mother's second-floor sitting room, Jessie's parterre evokes a stained-glass Romanesque cathedral window. She imitated the stained-glass panes with beds of single-colored flowers and used closely cropped privet hedges to serve as the leading. The garden has been restored and replanted with updated

hybrids of turn-of-the-century flowers, including lilies and daylilies, salvia, Veronicrastum, feverfew, and shasta daisies. The surrounding borders are planted with the property's original peonies, whose ample blossoms fill the garden with color in June. Dahlias add color in August. Behind the pergola, a hedge of white hydrangea creates a serene background for the vivid garden.

The Cutting and Kitchen Gardens at Hildene once provided all of the fruit, vegetables, and flowers for the Lincoln household. They have been replanted, and the paths and arbors have been restored. A cage protects blueberries, strawberries, currants, and raspberries from birds and other wildlife. An observation garden identifies and catalogs Hildene's original peony plants. A butterfly garden is used for youth education programs.

In addition to the mansion and gardens, you can visit twelve other historic buildings including the observatory, the Welcome Center and Museum Store in the historic carriage barn, the 1903 Pullman car Sunbeam, and a solar-powered goat dairy and cheese-making facility.

Walker Farm

1190 US Route 5, East Dummerston, VT 05346
(802) 254-2051
walkerfarm.com

HOURS: Daily 10–6

AMENITIES: 🏪

EVENTS: Garden seminars

Bountiful fields stretch out behind the greenhouses at this farm-turned-nursery, which has been in the Manix family since 1770. Karen and Jack Manix have operated the farm for 38 years, and left behind its long history of sheep and dairy farming to raise organic vegetables and unusual trees, shrubs, perennials, and annuals.

Walker Farm offers a wide variety of certified organic vegetable plant selections: more than 125 heirloom tomato varieties, 57 hot peppers, 20 types of eggplant, 21 choices for lettuce, common and uncommon herbs, Asian and Hispanic vegetables, celeriac, shallot, ground husk cherry starts, and lots more. You will also find hundreds of flowering annual starts from seed houses such as Botanical Interests, Renee's, Johnny's and Hart's. There is a nice selection of perennials arranged on tables by color and light requirements. The Manixes offer unique trees and shrubs for sale, including miniature conifers as well as variegated and weeping varieties of popular trees such as dogwoods, redbuds, and spruces. Your garden will never taste or look better!

The Walker Farm store offers an incredible bounty of organic vegetables and fruits, including some of the newest hybrids—cucamelons, button onions, Shishito Japanese peppers, and Honey Nut squash. The store also sells lovely bouquets of fresh flowers from the acres of cutting gardens behind the nursery.

Cider Hill Gardens & Gallery

1747 Hunt Rd., Windsor, VT 05089
(802) 674-6825
ciderhillgardens.com

HOURS: May–June: Wed.–Sun. 10–5; July–Sept.: Thurs.–Sun. 10–5

AMENITIES:

EVENTS: Tours for groups

Founded by gardeners Sarah and Gary Milek in 1974, Cider Hill Gardens Nursery and Gallery in historic Windsor offers a unique combination of gardens and fine art. Sarah manages the nursery, greenhouses, and display gardens, and Gary creates paintings and prints of the flowers that they grow.

Cider Hill Gardens was an abandoned apple orchard that the Mileks purchased and transformed into their home, garden, studio, and gallery. The nursery specializes in peonies, daylilies, and hostas, and you will find many varieties of these to choose from, in addition to other perennials for sun and shade. In the last few years the Mileks have become focused on gardens that support birds and native pollinators, and they are growing and stocking plants to support native wildlife. If

you are interested in starting a butterfly garden, Sarah will gladly tell you how to begin and which plants are most attractive to pollinators.

The display gardens at Cider Hill illustrate the couple's backgrounds in the arts. The plantings of blooming and foliage plants complement the flow of the landscape and create rhythms with their repeated forms and colors. Large beds feature hundreds of gorgeous, mature hostas, interplanted with colorful flowers and accented by statuary. You will also find growing fields of daylilies. After strolling through the display gardens, visit the gallery that houses Gary's award-winning paintings and prints of the brilliant flowers in the garden.

Saint Gaudens National Historic Site

139 St. Gaudens Rd., Cornish, NH 03745
(603) 675-2175
nps.gov/saga/index.htm

AREA: 370 acres

HOURS: Memorial Day–Oct 31: daily 9–4:30, grounds till dusk; Nov–May grounds open daily 9–4, exhibits closed

ADMISSION: $10

AMENITIES:

EVENTS: Guided tours, sculpture workshops, junior ranger program, summer concerts

Augustus Saint-Gaudens was the most renowned American sculptor of his day, and his home, gardens, and studios are preserved at the Saint-Gaudens National Historic Site.

Saint-Gaudens purchased the property in 1885 at the urging of his friend Charles Cotesworth Beaman, Jr., who owned the nearby Blow-Me-Down Farm (now also part of the historic site). The artist named the spot Aspet after his father's birthplace in France, built a studio, and encouraged his friends and fellow artists to join him in rural New Hampshire. Attracted by the area's natural beauty, about 100 artists, sculptors, writers, designers, and politicians settled there either full-time or during summers, and they frequently gathered at the Saint-Gaudens home. Some of the best-known members of the group were sculptor Daniel Chester French, painter Maxfield Parrish, painter

Frederic Remington, landscape designer Ellen Biddle Shipman, dancer Isadora Duncan, and architect and landscape designer Charles Platt. The artists' residences were connected via walking paths, and the area became known as the Cornish Art Colony, which flourished from the late 1800s to the 1920s .

You will find more than 100 of Saint-Gaudens' prominent works at Aspet, including the *Standing Lincoln,* the *Farragut Monument,* the *Shaw Memorial*, and *Diana*, cameo and bronze relief portraits of many notable individuals, and gold coins commissioned by Teddy Roosevelt. A gilded-bronze cast of *Amor Caritas* is installed in the atrium court and reflected in the pool. Saint-Gaudens hired architects to design the bases and landscapes for his sculptures, and his works are beautifully sited on the grounds of his home.

Saint-Gaudens was personally involved in all aspects of planning and developing the landscape around the house. At one time, the grounds included a golf course, bowling green, and swimming pool. The formal gardens are Italian in inspiration—divided by pine, hemlock, and yew hedges and accented with fountains and pools. Terraced flower gardens are planted with old-fashioned perennials in a scheme designed by Ellen Biddle Shipman. The Pan Grove is an outdoor room, featuring a green marble pool set in a birch grove with a statue of the Greek god Pan.

Toward the back of the house, off of the kitchen, the old vegetable garden has been converted into a cutting garden planted with historic varieties of annuals that are used for flower arrangements in the house. Look for the twig version of *Diana* among the tall flowers.

Aspet became the first National Park site in New Hampshire in 1965, and is the only site in the federal park system devoted to a visual artist.

Tarbin Gardens

321 Salisbury Rd., Franklin, NH 03235
(603) 934-3518
tarbingardens.com

AREA: 5 acres
HOURS: May–Sept.: Tues.–Sun. 10–6; open holiday Mondays
ADMISSION: $9
AMENITIES: 👫 🍼 ✕ 👶
EVENTS: Authentic English Cream Teas, June–Sept. 1–5 pm

Richard Tarbin and his mother, Jacky, have brought a little of their British homeland to Franklin, where you can stroll through a 5-acre garden and then enjoy an English cream tea. The Tarbins began transforming their heavily wooded property in 1973, cutting down trees; removing rocks and stumps; amending the soil with manure from their pigs, goats, and cattle; and planting the first gardens. Their home-based business evolved from selling annuals and hothouse tomatoes, to landscaping design and installation. Meanwhile, their own garden grew into a showplace. When friends and civic organizations began asking to tour their property, the Tarbins decided to open their garden to the public.

Tarbin Gardens is a series of themed spaces and microclimates that feature an amazing collection of plants. The Formal Garden has an English feel with hemlock hedges, urns on stone pediments, and a flagstone walk called "Winston Way" that leads to a grapevine-covered arbor. The walk is lined with hostas, astilbes, roses, lilies, and colorful annuals. The Alpine Slope features heaths and heathers, sun-loving prostrate evergreens, alpines, and tree peonies. The Three Pines Garden is planted with perennials that tolerate dry shade, including lamiums, woodland phlox, and heucheras. The Bog Garden is home to moisture-loving native plants, along with frogs and other wildlife. Richard has constructed four ponds throughout the gar-

den, some with waterfalls and koi. There are also other animals for children to enjoy: pigmy and dwarf Nigerian goats, Scottish Highland cattle, a hinny (cross between pony and donkey), and chickens live in the Barnyard, and parrots reside in outdoor cages next to the Succulent House. A tropical greenhouse, complete with a waterfall and pond, is crammed with orchids, night-blooming cereus, bromeliads, and tropical vines.

After a garden tour, the Rose Garden Patio is a welcome spot to relax, sip tea and enjoy a freshly baked scone. A small fountain adds the soothing sound of splashing water, and flowers perfume the air. It is a wonderful way to end your tour.

The Fells

456 NH-103A, Newbury, NH 03255
(603) 763-4789
thefells.org

AREA: 84 acres

HOURS: Gardens daily year round, 9–5

ADMISSION: $8 grounds only, $10 house & gardens

AMENITIES: 🏛 👫 🏛

EVENTS: Guided garden tours, mid June–mid August, Wed–Sun, 11 am; house tours; various programs

Named after the Scottish word for rocky upland pastures, The Fells is situated on a hillside overlooking scenic Lake Sunapee. It is the former summer home of American writer and diplomat John Milton Hay. Born in 1838, Hay served as Abraham Lincoln's private secretary and ambassador to Great Britain, and Secretary of State under presidents William McKinley and Theodore Roosevelt. To escape public life, in 1888 he and his wife, Clara Louise Stone, purchased nearly 1,000 acres on the shores of Lake Sunapee and built a colonial revival, gambrel-roofed house with a long open porch that looked out at rocky pastures.

The gardens at The Fells originate with the Hays' son Clarence and his wife, Alice Appleton Hay, who inherited the property in 1905. Clarence and Alice had traveled extensively, and brought a vision of formal European gardens to The Fells. Over several decades, they transformed it into a stately country home with terraced lawns and formal gardens. Clarence studied landscape architecture at Harvard, and created his first formal walled perennial garden, which gradually became a shady retreat surrounded by massive rhododendrons. The Hays added a stonewalled entry court with yew hedges, boxwood, and lilacs on the east side of the house. On the west side, they built a 100-foot-long stone wall that provides a backdrop for a dazzling perennial border with old-fashioned favorites such as iris, delphinium, hollyhocks, phlox, peonies and filipendula. On the south side of the house, they planted a rose garden enclosed

by high stone walls swathed in climbing hydrangea, wisteria, and espaliered pears. Water cascades from an urn fountain within a niche in the wall. Overlooking the lake, Clarence also established a Heather Bed, which was recently renovated and contains 20 varieties of heather.

Clarence developed a strong interest in rock gardens and alpine plants, and with a crew of stonemasons constructed a large rock garden to resemble a native New Hampshire hillside. He planted close to 600 different species and cultivars of plants, and kept meticulous notes on their cultural information and cultivations. Some of his plants are still in the garden, and many more have been added, including prostrate conifers, asclepsias, primroses, and sedums. Stone paths and a stream wind through the garden, and lead to a lily pool surrounded by lady's mantle, ferns, and Japanese iris. Stone Japanese lanterns give the garden an Asian feel.

Bedrock Gardens

45 High Rd., Lee, NH 03861
(603) 659-2993
bedrockgardens.org

AREA: 20 acres

HOURS: May–Sept.: 1st and 3rd weekend of the month; Columbus Day weekend: Sat.–Sun. 10–4

ADMISSION: $10 suggested donation

AMENITIES: 👥

EVENTS: Art shows, concerts, fairy & hobbit festival

Bedrock Gardens is a 20-acre garden that Carol Stocker of the *Boston Globe* aptly described as a "cross between Sissinghurst and the Dr. Seuss Sculpture Garden." In 1980 Bob Munger and Jill Nooney purchased this former dairy farm and began a 30-year transformation of the landscape into a collection of themed garden rooms enlivened by whimsical sculptures.

Nooney is a practicing clinical social worker, as well as an artist and graduate of the Radcliffe Institute Landscape Design program. She uses old farm equipment and repurposed metal to create a variety of abstract sculptures, arches, arbors, water features and "creatures" inspired by nature and her imagination. Munger is a retired doctor and a lifelong tinkerer. Nooney is the garden's visionary artist and "problem maker." He is the "problem solver," the implementor of those visions, including beautifully patterned walkways and patios, and hydraulics for water features.

Nooney and Munger created their garden as a journey with "places to go, places to pause and rest, and interesting things to see along the way." Nearly two-dozen "points of interest," many with humorous names, are connected by paths that wind through garden rooms, around ponds, and through woodlands.

Closest to the house, a yew hedge encloses a formal parterre planted with white flowers, with a diamond patterned bluestone path and a circular pool and fountain. The Straight and Narrow garden features a cobbled-edged path that runs between beds of native trees, shrubs, and perennials. The Swaleway's woodland wildflowers welcome spring amidst towers of balanced stones. The Garish Garden's playful sculptures fit in with flowers in flaming reds and oranges and trees and shrubs with bright gold foliage.

Bedrock Gardens is full of new ideas for gardeners as well as new takes on classic garden forms. The Wiggle Waggle is a wavy 200-foot long water channel, planted with lotus and water lilies. The Spiral Garden is a "twist" on a traditional maze garden, with twirling roof ventilators on spiral stands that emphasize the Fibonacci-inspired paving laid in a moss floor. Grass Acre is a "painting" of Switchgrass, Hakone Grass, and Little Blue Stem, anchored by a metal sculpture that evokes a mountain range. The Dark Woods is a grove of dead trees accented with sculptural ghosts, spiders, and other scary creatures. The Wave is a series of 26 small metal characters on pedestals backed by a tall arborvitae hedge. Several ponds and many more gardens await the visitor.

Walking through the gardens is a delightful journey. There are many places to sit and enjoy a vista or a sculpture along the way. The Japanese Garden and Tea House offer quiet repose in the woods, and the two thrones at the Termi at the far end of the large pond offer a stunning view along the 900-foot axis through the garden. Nooney has designed the garden with an artist's eye and her strategic placement of focal points and vistas takes classical garden design concepts into a contemporary setting.

Nooney and Munger want to preserve the garden for future generations and are working with Friends of Bedrock Gardens and new executive director John Forti to transition the property into a public garden.

Celia Thaxter's Garden

Appledore Island, off the coast of New Hampshire
(603) 862-5346
shoalsmarinelaboratory.org/event/celia-thaxters-garden-tours

AREA: 15' x 50' cutting garden; Island is 95 acres total

HOURS: Available through guided tours only; about 8 per year, late June–early August; registration required

ADMISSION: $50 or $100 depending on tour

AMENITIES:

Celia Laighton Thaxter was a notable 19th-century writer who summered on Appledore Island in the Isles of Shoals, a group of nine islands located 10 miles off the coast of Maine and New Hampshire. The garden she created there was the site of an informal summer "salon" on the island.

Thaxter grew up on the Isles of Shoals and returned to become innkeeper at her family's resort hotel on Appledore Island. When her parents died, she moved to their nearby cottage and created a 15- by 50-foot cutting garden of seasonal flowers for use in the hotel and the cottage. Thaxter had loved gardening from the time she was a child, when she started her first seedlings in eggshells. Her cutting garden included sweet peas, poppies, marigolds, peonies, larkspur, cleome, heliotrope, roses, calendulas, and dozens of other flowers planted in raised beds in front of her porch.

Thaxter's garden became a focal point of cultural life at Appledore, providing a rich source of artistic inspiration for herself and her friends. She wrote poetry and prose with naturalistic themes and painted china, decorative tiles, and watercolors with floral motifs. Her parlor was a studio, salesroom, and salon where she hosted friends, including Ralph Waldo Emerson, Nathaniel Hawthorne, Sarah Orne Jewett, William Morris Hunt, and Childe Hassam. Appledore functioned as a retreat for New England artists from the middle of the 1870s until Thaxter's death in 1894, and it became an important prototype for later American art colonies.

In 1894, Houghton Mifflin posthumously published Thaxter's most famous book, *An Island Garden*. Part journal and part handbook, the text is illustrated by Childe Hassam. It contains his 1892 masterpiece *In the Garden*, showing Thaxter as she gardened, hatless in a long white dress, standing in bright sunlight among her poppies, hollyhocks, and other flowers.

"Of all the wonderful things in the wonderful

of her original daylilies and hop vines. Since then, each year about 1,000 heirloom plants are grown to maturity in greenhouses at University of New Hampshire. They are ferried to Appledore, where a small group of volunteers plants them in carefully prepared beds in time for the first visitors to arrive. Some of the heirloom seeds are no longer available in the US, and are collected from all over the world. Certain plants, like the poppies and asters, are sown three separate times, so that they can be seen in bloom all summer. Most of the original buildings, including Thaxter's cottage, the hotel, and artist studios were swept away in a fire in 1914. Celia's porch was reconstructed in 2017, and provides a faithful setting for her garden.

universe of God," Thaxter wrote, "nothing seems to me more surprising than the planting of a seed in the blank earth and result thereof."

Since 1966, the Shoals Marine Laboratory, operated by Cornell and the University of New Hampshire, has used Appledore Island for summer marine biology programs. In 1977, Cornell professor John Kingsbury reconstructed Thaxter's garden based on her 1893 plan, using the same annuals and vines that she had planted, and some

There are two options for seeing the garden: Celia Thaxter's Garden Tour, which includes round-trip boat transportation, a garden tour, and catered lunch for $100; and the Appledore Island Walking Tour, with boat transportation, and walking tours of the island focused on the cultural history, and natural history. You must bring your own lunch, and the cost is $50. Both tours require advance registration, and sell out early in the season.

Rundlet-May House

364 Middle St., Portsmouth, NH 03801
(603) 430-7531
historicnewengland.org/property/rundlet-may-house/

AREA: 2 acres

HOURS: June 1–Oct. 15: first & third Saturdays 11–4; closed July 4

ADMISSION: $8

AMENITIES:

Merchant James Rundlet moved to Portsmouth in 1794 and made a fortune manufacturing textiles. He built this Federal style house on a terraced rise outside of the busy commercial district for his wife and 13 children. The house showcased the finest furnishings, wall coverings, and latest innovations available at the time. It remained in the Rundlet-May family for four generations, until it was deeded to Historic New England by James' great-grandson Ralph in 1971.

The grounds surrounding the house illustrate James Rundlet's orderly bent. Fences and shrub hedges clearly delineate the formal terraces, paths, garden beds, and extensive fruit orchards. The property's archives include the original landscape plan as well as the records of poplar and pear trees, grapevines, and roses that Rundlet chose for his garden. In the late 1800s, Mary Ann Robins May updated the garden with plants popular at the time and added the spiral trellises that were popular in Portsmouth.

Today, the gardens retain their original layout with plantings that were fashionable during the Colonial Revival period. Rectangular lawns are enclosed by beds of violet poppies, periwinkle love-in-a-mist, pink phlox, nicotiana, Queen Anne's lace, and variegated euphorbia. Dozens of peonies bloom in June, roses envelop a crisp white pergola, and an apple orchard bears fruit in the back of the garden.

Another Historic New England property in Portsmouth is the Governor John Langdon House, located at 143 Pleasant St. John Langdon was a merchant, shipbuilder, Revolutionary War general, signer of the Constitution, and three-term governor of New Hampshire. The house is open for tours, and the formal garden features a twelve-foot deep perennial border and a beautiful 100-foot arbor covered with climbing roses and grapevines. See historicnewengland.org/property/governor-john-langdon-house/ for more information.

Moffatt-Ladd House & Garden

154 Market St, Portsmouth, NH 03801
(603) 436-8221
moffattladd.org

AREA: 1 acre
HOURS: June 1–Oct. 15: Mon.–Sat. 11–4, Sun. 1–5
ADMISSION: $8, garden only $2
AMENITIES:
EVENTS: House tours, museum talks, various events

John Moffatt, one of the wealthiest men in the New Hampshire colony, built this historic house for his son, Samuel, in 1763. The Georgian mansion was the tallest and grandest of its day in Portsmouth, with a view of the family wharves on the Piscataqua River. Samuel was ruined financially and the house passed to his sister Katharine. Katharine married General William Whipple, who served as a Portsmouth delegate to the Revolutionary Assembly and a representative to the Continental Congress. Since the Whipples were among the most prominent people in the New Hampshire colony, the home was a likely gathering place for Revolutionary patriots. William returned home after signing the Declaration of Independence in

1776 with a handful of horse chestnuts that he had picked up in Philadelphia, and planted one in the yard to commemorate the momentous event. The tree still stands, and was named the "Millennium Landmark Tree" for the State of New Hampshire in 2000.

John Moffatt's great grandson, Alexander Hamilton Ladd, a successful cotton trader, lived in the house from 1862 to 1900. He created the beautiful terraced formal garden that exists at the Moffatt-Ladd house today. Ladd kept a garden journal with meticulous records of the garden's layout and his plant purchases. Although the garden is only one acre in size, it appears much larger, with a 300-foot axis path leading from the house up four terraces to a wrought-iron gate at the rear boundary. Unusual grass steps lead from the first level to the upper flowerbeds. Gravel paths wind through rose arbors and borders planted with daylilies, martagon lilies, phlox, dahlias, helianthus, and other perennials. Ladd loved tulips and other spring flowers, and in one year he noted that bad weather had caused him to lose 60,000 bulbs.

As you stroll through the garden, notice the wisteria trellises mounted on the back of the house. The helical trellises that support old roses are an unusual design distinctive to Portsmouth. An English damask rose planted in 1768 by Sarah Catherine Mason Moffatt still blooms in June. Ladd established the beehives to ensure that his flowers would be properly pollinated. Curved white benches throughout the garden invite you to relax and enjoy the flowers.

The house remained within the Moffat-Ladd family for nearly 150 years, and upon Ladd's death, his heirs offered it to The National Society of the Colonial Dames of America in the State of New Hampshire to be preserved as a museum.

Prescott Park

1 Water St., Portsmouth, NH 03801
(603) 431-8748
prescottparknh.org

AREA: 10 acres
HOURS: Daily, dawn to dusk
ADMISSION: Free
AMENITIES:
GPS address: 105 Marcy St.

Prescott Park is a garden gem located on the banks of the Piscataqua River in the heart of Portsmouth. It is the creation of two sisters, Portsmouth public school teachers Josie and Mary Prescott, who had the vision and goodwill to create this beautiful waterfront area. Starting in 1932, when their brother, Charles, left them a fortune, the sisters purchased parcels of land along the Piscataqua, developed them, and deeded the land to the city along with a sizeable trust fund to establish a park. The resulting 10-acre park has five distinct areas, with municipal docks, three boardwalk piers, a performing amphitheater and stage, formal gardens, historic buildings, trial gardens, and Four Tree Island, a prime spot for picnics and views of the harbor.

The formal Josie Prescott Memorial Garden was designed in 1965 by Moriece and Gary Inc. Landscape Architects of Cambridge, Mass. Eight pink crabapples, along with maples, gingko, and magnolia trees, provide the structure of the gar-

den. Brick pathways connect three circular pools complete with fountains, and white benches on the periphery allow for relaxing and enjoying the colorful display of flowers. Daffodils, hyacinths, and tulips burst forth in spring, and lead to an amazing summer display of coleus, rudbeckia, daylilies, zinnias, and grasses. Surrounding the garden are more ornamental trees, including franklinia, stewartia, weeping katsuras, and Chinese fringe trees.

The All-American trial gardens were established in 1975 on the south side of the park. The display showcases new varieties of annuals suitable for Portsmouth's climate. The gardens were originally a collaboration between Prescott Park and the University of New Hampshire. Nearly 40 garden beds were dug and planted, and UNH students provided some of the ongoing maintenance as part of their course of studies. The current park superintendent was one of those students, and today park staff continue to plant and maintain the area, with about 400 flowering plants donated annually by UNH. Local nurseries supply and donate the many hundreds of gorgeous flowers blooming in the park.

Strawberry Banke

14 Hancock St., Portsmouth, NH 03801
(603) 433-1100
strawberybanke.org

AREA: 10 acres
HOURS: May–Oct.: daily 10–5
ADMISSION: $19.50
AMENITIES:
EVENTS: Many special events throughout the year

Strawberry Banke is a living history museum that preserves the people, buildings, and gardens in Portsmouth's South End neighborhood. Captain Walter Neale built a settlement in this area in 1630, and named it after the wild berries growing along the Piscataqua River. Strawberry Banke has existed as a neighborhood for almost 400 years. It opened as a museum in 1965 with 37 restored buildings. Ten houses with furnished historic interiors are open to the public, while the remainder are private homes. There are also formal exhibits on archaeology, architecture, post-and-beam construction, woodworking tools and skills.

Garden Design magazine recently recognized Strawberry Banke as one of four sites in the world that teach about evolving landscapes. Each of six historic gardens at Strawberry Banke illustrates a different era in the settlement's history. Each is in its original location and exhibits plants and planting techniques of its time, based on meticulous research. The oldest is the Shelburne 17th Century Kitchen Garden, with raised beds supplying produce and medicinal and culinary herbs outside the kitchen door. It is one of the most authentic recreations of a colonial era garden, based on written records and archaeological exploration of the site.

The 18th century Walsh House Teaching Garden illustrates the introduction of more ornamentals, which were often brought back to America from mercantile sailing voyages, and include lilacs, peonies, irises, daylilies, and roses.

The 19th century is captured in the Goodwin Garden, with its formal gardens bedded out with annuals in the Victorian style, and fashionable plants imported from around the world. The garden also features a recently renovated historic hothouse housing exotic tropicals appropriate to 1870.

Three different gardens illustrate the changes of the 20th century. The 1908 Colonial Revival Garden is a memorial to author Thomas Bailey Aldrich. Set next to the Aldrich House where he grew up, the garden is formal, with brick pathways and a summerhouse. The Shapiro Ukrainian Vegetable Garden is representative of the many small urban gardens planted by immigrants in the 20th century Puddle Dock neighborhood. These gardens were used to propagate heirloom vegetables that were important in the family's traditional cuisine. The Victory Garden recalls WWII, when home vegetable gardens supplied Americans with not only fruits and vegetables, but also poultry for eggs and meat. At their height, Victory Gardens accounted for nearly half of all fresh produce grown in the country.

In addition to orchards, there are three other teaching gardens at Strawberry Banke: an herb garden, a Victorian children's garden, and a community garden. The Horticulture Center in Cotton Tenant House provides seasonal programs related to gardening, food preservation, and the use of plants grown in Strawberry Banke gardens.

Fuller Gardens

10 Willow Ave., North Hampton, NH 03862
(603) 964-5414
fullergardens.org

AREA: 2.5 acres

HOURS: May 15–Oct 15: daily 10–5:30

ADMISSION: $9

AMENITIES:

EVENTS: Annual Mother's Day Weekend Plant Sale, Annual Garden Party

Roses are the main event at Fuller Gardens. Now a test garden for the American Rose Society, it showcases more than 1,200 rose bushes. The 125 varieties have staggered bloom times, so there is color from June until October.

Fuller Gardens began as Runnymede-by-the-Sea, the summer estate of Bostonians Alvan and Viola Fuller. Alvan was a self-made businessman, art collector, philanthropist, and politician who served as governor of Massachusetts in the 1920s. The original landscape was designed by Arthur A. Shurtleff, but the garden evolved and was enlarged over the years, with the help of the Olmstead Brothers firm of Boston. The front garden was designed as the estate's showpiece in 1938. It was meant to be appreciated from the street and utilized a "false perspective," in which the back of the garden is narrower than the front, making the space appear longer than it actually is. The Fullers rarely frequented the garden themselves, but they enjoyed viewing it from the upstairs bedroom windows and welcomed the public. The front garden was planted with hundreds of roses in formal parterre beds, and surrounded by hedges and flower borders filled with coneflowers, astilbe, salvias, baptisia, and geraniums. Statuary and tuteurs draped with clematis punctuated the hedges.

In addition to the front garden, you will find a second rose garden is laid out in a circular pattern surrounding a central antique wellhead. It is enclosed by a privet hedge and a cedar fence upon which are trained espaliered apple trees. A

shady Japanese garden provides a quiet sanctuary, with paths leading through hostas, ferns, azaleas, mountain laurel, and rhododendrons surrounding a pool filled with giant koi. Near the remaining carriage house, a glass conservatory houses tropical plants, begonias, and vines. A large display bed of dahlias provides stunning color in late summer.

The gardens are meticulously maintained by a knowledgeable staff headed by director Jamie Colen. The roses are protected from harsh winter temperatures with buckets of soil heaped upon their crowns in early December. Instead of using mulch to suppress weeds, the staff weed the beds twice a week and pay careful attention to soil quality, amending it regularly with compost and lime. As a result, the roses are healthy and vigorous, with few pests and almost no diseases, so chemical treatments are unnecessary. As they age and need to be replaced, new roses are purchased from Roseland Nurseries in Acushnet, Massachusetts. The colorful gardens continue to delight the public as they did almost 100 years ago, and the Fullers are probably happily watching from above.

Mason Hollow Nursery

47 Scripts Ln., Mason, NH 03048
(603) 878-4347
masonhollow.com

HOURS: Mid-May–Sept
AMENITIES:

Located off the beaten path in the small town of Mason lies Mason Hollow Nursery, a paradise for hosta collectors and garden enthusiasts.

Owners Sue and Chuck Andersen opened Mason Hollow in 2001 as a labor of love—love of hostas, that is. Chuck had long been interested in horticulture, having started his first job in a greenhouse at age 14. He developed passions for orchids and hostas, and became very active in the New England and American hosta societies. Mason Hollow now offers more than 800 varieties of hosta—including cultivars introduced by local hybridizers such as Rick Goodenough of Massachusetts—that you will not find elsewhere. You can see mature specimens in the display gardens surrounding the nursery.

In addition to hosta, the Andersens offer heucheras and other shade plants. Garden railway enthusiasts will find wonderful dwarf conifers, ferns, sedums, and other miniature perennials that fit perfectly in a garden railway setting. The hothouse at Mason Hollow displays a unique collection of about 2,000 varieties of orchids in every shape, size, and color. While these are not available for sale, they are definitely worth a look! Some are smaller than a thumbnail, and many do not resemble any orchids you might know. It is amazing to see these orchids from all corners of the world—from the hot tropics to cold mountain ranges—sharing a cozy home in New Hampshire.

Pickity Place

248 Nutting Hill Rd., Mason, NH 03048
(603) 878-1151
pickityplace.com

GRANDMOTHER'S HOUSE
BUILT IN 1786, THIS COTTAGE WAS USED BY ELIZABETH ORTON J. TO ILLUSTRATE HER VERSION THE BOOK LITTLE RED RIDING

AREA: 5 acres

HOURS: April–Dec.: daily 10–5; Jan.–March: daily 10–4; closed holidays

AMENITIES:

EVENTS: Five-course herbal luncheon with daily seatings at 11:30, 12:45, 2:00; reservations recommended

Built in 1786, Pickity Place is a literal storybook cottage with greenhouses, a gift shop, and a restaurant that serves gourmet luncheons inspired by its gardens.

When Elizabeth Orton Jones was called upon by Little Golden Books to illustrate the 1948 edition of *Little Red Riding Hood*, she chose the nearby red Cape Cod-style house as the model for grandmother's house. The current owners of Pickity Place have fun with the property's claim to fame. You can peek into a replica of "Grandmother's Bedroom" complete with the Big Bad Wolf, and purchase many Little Red Riding Hood mementos.

Pickity Place is a haven for gardeners, foodies, and storybook lovers. It is famous for its five-course gourmet luncheon, which features fresh herbs and edible flowers harvested daily from the kitchen gardens. The menu changes monthly, and reservations are highly recommended. After the delicious meal, you can wander through more than five acres of culinary and flower gardens complete with old-fashioned bee skeps, birdhouses, and meandering brick pathways. The rustic old barn is home to an Herb Shop chock-full of gift items, aromatic scents, baking mixes, kitchen accents, gourmet goodies, and treats for your pet. A second barn contains a Garden Shop and Greenhouse, with herbs and perennials for sale.

Hamilton House

40 Vaughans Ln., South Berwick, ME 03908
(207) 384-5269
historicnewengland.org/property/hamilton-house/

AREA: 50 acres

HOURS: June 1–Oct. 15: Wed.–Sun. 11–4

ADMISSION: $10

AMENITIES:

EVENTS: House tours on the hour. Sunday afternoon concerts beginning July 4

In the late 1700s, when the Salmon Falls River was a bustling center of commerce, shipping merchant Jonathan Hamilton built his grand Georgian mansion on a bluff overlooking his wharf. A century later, the house, decrepit but largely unchanged, went on the market. Writer Sarah Orne Jewett, who lived nearby, convinced her friend Emily Tyson of Boston to purchase the house. Tyson and her stepdaughter Elise fell in love with the elegant house and the area. Like other members of their society, they were enamored with the romance of owning a Colonial-era country house, which provided a healthy summer retreat away from the heat and pollution of their city home.

The Tysons set about restoring the house to its original glory. They commissioned artist George Porter Fernald to cover the walls of the dining room and parlor with fanciful murals depicting their travels abroad and local landmarks, including Hamilton's ships being unloaded onto wharves in front of Hamilton House. The country home became a gathering place for Boston's intellectual circle, and hosted many elaborate parties.

Passionate gardeners, the Tysons created a Colonial Revival garden on the estate. The garden was designed as a series of rooms surrounded by trellises and a pergola. The classical lines of the garden extended from a water trench that ran from the well to the house. The garden rooms were planted with old-fashioned flowers such as peonies, globe thistle, Asian lilies, day-lilies, phlox, nigella, and foxglove, and adorned with period garden ornaments and millstones.

Elise Tyson Vaughan bequeathed Hamilton House and its gardens, outbuildings, and surrounding fields to Historic New England in 1949. In the 1990s, Historic New England began a restoration of the gardens, which continues today. Although the Tysons did not keep a record of what was planted, Elise was an accomplished amateur photographer, and took many photos of the gardens and property. The gardens had also been featured several times in *House Beautiful* in the 1920s. These sources provided the blueprints for the design and planting of the gardens. The garden arch was rebuilt from Elise's photos and placed in its original location. Historic New England hopes some day to raise funds to rebuild the pergola, which was damaged in a hurricane and torn down in the 1950s. Today, the gardens at Hamilton House are lovingly cared for by devoted volunteers, and are a beautiful place to visit and admire the Colonial Revival style in New England.

Snug Harbor Farm

87 Western Ave., Kennebunk, ME 04043
(207) 967-2414
snugharborfarm.com

AREA: 3 acres
HOURS: Daily 9–5
AMENITIES:
EVENTS: Topiary, container and floral design workshops

When sailors retire, they like to say that they're going to a snug harbor. The farm's first owner in 1850 was a Dutch sea captain who named the place. Tony Elliot purchased Snug Harbor Farm in 1998 to raise and collect unusual plant material for his landscape design clients. Maine's challenging topography, tough climate, and tricky growing seasons call for a unique design approach, one that Elliot calls the New England Farm Garden style. He creates defined garden rooms planted with heirloom and cultivated plants close to the house, and wilder, more organically planted spaces further out on the property. He uses indigenous stone and timeworn accessories to give his gardens an established look.

Snug Harbor reflects this New England Farm Garden style in its greenhouses, outbuildings, dovecotes, espaliers, plant selection, and nostalgic items offered for sale. Elliot loves the allure of chipped, tarnished, and rusted pieces, and his shop displays rusty trellises, aged statuary, mossy pots, terrariums, and stone vases. Elliott is famous for his extraordinary plants and unique presentation—particularly the elegant myrtle, lemon cypress, rosemary, and fuscia topiaries displayed in hand-thrown terra-cotta pots that are designed especially for the farm. Elliott learned topiary from renowned horticulturist Allen Haskell, with whom he worked in the 1980s. The process is long and painstaking—the standards are staked, pruned, pinched and trimmed for 18 months prior to sale—but the resulting miniature topiary trees are absolutely magical.

Nickels-Sortwell House

121 Main St. (Route 1), Wiscasset, ME 04578
(207) 882-7169
historicnewengland.org/property/nickels-sortwell-house/

AREA: .5 acre

HOURS: June 1–Oct. 15: Fri.–Sun. 11–4; Sunken Garden open daily, dawn–dusk

ADMISSION: Garden, free; house $8

Nestled on the shores of the Sheepscot River, tiny Wiscasset justifiably calls itself the "prettiest village in Maine, " with a main street lined with sea captains' mansions, Federal and Victorian homes, an 1824 brick courthouse, and almost 30 antiques shops. The town owes some of its current charm to the preservationist efforts of Frances Sortwell, one of the owners of the Nickels-Sortwell House.

Nickels-Sortwell House has been the jewel of Wiscasset's Main Street since it was built by sea captain William Nickels at the peak of the town's prosperity in 1807. Thomas Jefferson's Embargo of 1807 ruined Captain Nickels financially, and the mansion was purchased in 1899 by successful industrialist and former mayor of Cambridge, Massachusetts, Alvin Sortwell, as a summer home for his large family. His wife, Gertrude, and daughter, Frances, lovingly restored the house, decorating it in the Colonial Revival style. Known for her wit and sparkling personality, Frances became Wiscasset's most dynamic preservationist. She purchased and restored eight historic houses and several public buildings in town, including a former bank building that she donated for use by the Wiscasset Library.

Next to the Nickels-Sortwell House, you can enjoy another of the Sortwells' preservation projects, at the former location of the Hilton House Hotel, which burned to the ground in 1903. Frances and Gertrude bought the property and put the hotel's stone foundation to good use. With the help of Frances' friend Rose Ishbel Greeley, the first female graduate of Harvard's landscape architecture program, they transformed the dismal site into a beautiful and tranquil sunken garden, which the family used for many years as a place for quiet contemplation and outdoor entertaining.

Enclosed by hedges of rhododendrons and lilacs, the sunken garden is a "secret garden" in bustling Wiscasset. Brick walkways outline formal flowerbeds planted with tulips, peonies, Siberian iris, ferns, phlox, and hostas. Stone benches and tables provide restful areas for reading a book or having a picnic. It is a quiet respite and an elegant monument to the woman who preserved Wiscasset's history for generations to come.

The Sortwell family gave the mansion to Historic New England in 1956. It is open for touring, and its garden is in very early stages of restoration. The sunken garden was donated to Wiscasset, and has been maintained by the town and the Wiscasset Garden Club.

Coastal Maine Botanical Gardens

132 Botanical Gardens Dr., Boothbay, ME 04537
(207) 633-8000
mainegardens.org

AREA: 295 acres

HOURS: May 1–Oct. 31: daily 9–5; July–Aug. daily 9–6

ADMISSION: $16

AMENITIES:

EVENTS: Garden tours, boat tours, kayaking, many special events

The Coastal Maine Botanical Gardens opened to the public in 2007 after 16 years of planning, planting, and building. This ambitious project began with a group of mid-coast Maine residents who decided that northern New England was in need of a botanical garden. In 1996, after an extensive search, the founders purchased 128 acres in Boothbay, using their own homes as collateral. With its diverse natural ecosystems, dramatic topography, location on the Back River, and more than 300 native plant species already on the site, the property was ideal.

Since then, Coastal Maine Botanical Gardens has grown to 295 acres, and welcomes more than 190,000 visitors annually. Its design is inspired by Maine's coastal landscape, and it showcases the

work of local artisans and the use of local materials. Under the direction of executive director Bill Cullina, the garden exhibits exquisite plantings, creative garden spaces, elegant structures, and fine art, all set within a stunning natural landscape.

The Lerner Garden of the Five Senses is a special garden designed for horticultural therapy, offering mental and physical stimulation through the senses of sight, sound, smell, touch, and taste. The garden beds are waist-high, extended, and have railings for handicapped access. The sounds come from breezes passing through the plants. There are fragrant flowers and herbs to smell, plants with textured foliage to touch, and easy-to-harvest vegetables such as greens and cherry tomatoes to taste.

The two-acre Children's Garden is delightful for children and adults alike. It was designed by landscape architect Herb Schall and uses themes from children's literature. Among the whimsical plantings, you will encounter playful statuary of bears and Peter Rabbit's coat. Garden spaces include a maze, a pond with a fishing dock, a vegetable garden, a keeper's cottage and story barn, chicken coop, spray fountains, a bog with carnivorous plants, tree house and more. The garden is lively with the sound of children's laughter. A trail leads from the Children's Garden to the shore and Fairy House Village, where kids can create fairy houses from twigs, leaves, and pinecones.

Coastal Maine features a series of trails throughout the woods including several that lead to the Rhododendron Garden, the Meditation Garden, and the Pier. The Meditation Garden is tucked into the woods on the Shoreland Trail. The garden is Japanese in style, with granite stonework and a great basin that evokes the ebb and flow of the sea. Shade loving plants create a beautiful tapestry under the trees, and ocean views enhance the scene. The Rhododendron Garden is carved into a hill-

side with a dramatic waterfall. It can be reached by foot in about 35 minutes, or via shuttle.

In just 10 years, Coastal Maine has become one of the largest public gardens in the country. Plans are under way to expand the garden to accommodate the number of visitors, increase programming,

and expand horticultural research. The master plan includes a huge glass conservatory to house special plant shows in winter and spring, and surrounding gardens with a large pond, stream, and bog garden.

Coastal Maine Botanical Gardens

Massachusetts

SUGGESTED DAILY ITINERARIES

Morning
Highfield Hall & Gardens, Falmouth (2)
Lunch–Quarterdeck, Falmouth
Heritage Museums & Gardens, Sandwich (3)

Morning
Allen Haskell Park, New Bedford (6)
Avant Gardens, Dartmouth (4)
Lunch–Bayside, Westport
Sylvan Nusery, Westport (5)
Tranquil Lake Nursery, Rehoboth (7)

Morning
Longfellow House & Garden, Cambridge (13)
Mount Auburn Cemetery, Cambridge (14)
Lunch–Faneuil Hall
Rose Kennedy Greenway, Boston (12)

Morning
Arnold Arboretum, Boston (11)
Lunch–Blue Hills Grille, Canton
Eleanor Cabot Bradley Estate, Canton (9)
Cochato Nursery, Holbrook (10)
Briggs Nursery, North Attleboro (8)

Morning & Lunch
Tower Hill Botanic Garden, Boylston (23)

Morning
Stevens-Coolidge Place, North Andover (19)
Ropes Mansion, Salem (16)
Lunch–Gulu-Gulu Café, Salem
Sedgwick Long Hill Garden, Beverly (17)
Crane Estate, Ipswich (18)

Morning
The Gardens at Elm Bank, Wellesley (20)
Lunch–Legal Seafood, Framingham
Garden in the Woods, Framingham(21)
Weston Nurseries, Hopkinton (22)

Morning
Chesterwood, Stockbridge (27)
Lunch–Red Lion Inn, Stockbridge
Naumkeag, Stockbridge (28)

Morning
Bridge of Flowers, Shelburne Falls(25)
Lunch–West End Pub, Shelburne Falls
The Mount, Lenox (26)

Morning
Berkshire Botanical Garden, Stockbridge (29)
Lunch–Once upon a Table, Stockbridge
Ashintully, Tyringham (30)
Campo de'Fiori, Sheffield (31)

Massachusetts

Polly Hill Arboretum

809 State Rd., West Tisbury, MA 02575
(508) 693-9426
pollyhillarboretum.org

AREA: 72 acres
HOURS: Daily 9:30–4
ADMISSION: $5
AMENITIES:
EVENTS: Workshops, garden tours at 10 am, explorer backpacks for kids

If you're vacationing on Martha's Vineyard, be sure to visit this 72-acre public garden that showcases the results of 50 years of horticultural experimentation by founder Polly Hill, who died in 2007 at the age of 100. Set among stone walls and meadows are rare trees and shrubs from around the world, including Hill's own azaleas, the national stewartia collection, a kousa dogwood allée, and more. The Arboretum was recently added to the National Register of Historic Places, marking its evolution through 300 years of history.

Polly and her husband, Julian, took over her parents' farm property in the 1950s. A practical gardener who learned from trial and error, she found the Martha's Vineyard "horticulturally impoverished" and was determined to learn what else would grow in the island's soil and climate. At age 50, she began planting seeds and trying

cultivars that no one thought could survive on the Vineyard. She kept meticulous records, selected superior forms of her plants, and gave them cultivar names, ultimately naming nearly 80 plants with unique characteristics and making them available to the public.

Hill's life is an inspiration to gardeners and anyone who is determined to make a meaningful change in their life at any age. As she said, "Fifty is a great age to try something new." What she called her horticultural experiment has become her legacy—a historic landscape that has evolved into a public garden and scientific institution devoted to research, plant conservation, and exploration.

Stewartias, with their striking bark and elegant flowers, fascinated Hill. She sought out as many species as possible and grew them from seed. The Arboretum is home to over 70 stewartia trees representing 21 taxa with nine distinct cultivars introduced by Hill, and has been named a Nationally Accredited Plant Collection.

Magnolias were another favorite. She made several unique selections, including a splendid form of big-leaf magnolia that she named for her husband, *Magnolia macrophylla* 'Julian Hill.' In June this dramatic tree produces enormous white flowers amongst leaves that are nearly two-feet long! At the Arboretum, magnolias bloom from early March through early July, when the last blossoms of the evergreen southern magnolia open.

The largest plant collection at the Arboretum is of rhododendrons and azaleas, many of which were started from seeds collected in southeastern U.S. and Japan. These include Hill's North Tisbury azaleas, ground cover azaleas that grow to about 15" in height and are particularly well suited for rock gardens. Rhodies and azaleas bloom from March to September. A new two-acre woodland garden is being installed to accommodate the Arboretum's growing plant inventory.

Highfield Hall and Gardens

58 Highfield Dr., Falmouth, MA 02540
(508) 495-1878
highfieldhallandgardens.org

AREA: 15 acres

HOURS: Gardens: daily dawn–dusk; house: April 15–Oct. 31: Mon.–Fri. 10–4, Sat.–Sun. 10–2

ADMISSION: $5

AMENITIES:

EVENTS: Estate walks: Apr.–Oct.: 1st and 3rd Sundays 12:30–1:30; exhibits, concerts, classes and more

Highfield Hall and Gardens is the magnificently restored 1878 estate of the Beebe family, with a dramatic history and a vibrant present-day. It offers something for everyone—the gardener, history buff, antiques collector, art lover, theater fan, and nature lover.

Highfield Hall was one of two mansions built on nearly 700 acres owned by the James Beebe family, which gathered on Cape Cod for the summers and entertained in grand fashion. When the last Beebe died, the estate was sold and used for a variety of purposes by subsequent owners. In 1949, it was purchased by DeWitt TerHeun, a patron of the performing arts, who created a theater on the grounds to train student actors. The theater remains the home of Falmouth's much-loved summer stock College Light Opera Company from Oberlin College.

From the late 1970s to 1994, Highfield was abandoned and suffered two decades of neglect and vandalism. In 1994, the owners filed a demolition permit, which propelled a group of Falmouth citizens to organize to save the mansion. The group was embroiled in years of legal battles to stave off demolition. Volunteers cleared the property and secured the building from further decay and vandalism, while raising money and public awareness of the mansion's plight. Finally, in 2000, the Town of Falmouth took Highfield Hall and 6 acres by eminent domain, and authorized the non-profit group to renovate and operate the estate. The extraordinary restoration effort that followed was made possible through more than $8.5 million in donations, almost all from private individuals. In 2006 the first stage of restoration was completed, and Highfield opened to the public.

The Beebes were passionate about their landscape and enlisted renowned designers Ernest Bowditch and Frederick Law Olmstead to create formal gardens, a labyrinth, and walking paths that wind through a rhododendron dell, stands of heritage beech plantings, and nearly 400 acres of woodlands. Two formal gardens were part of the original plan. The West Garden was originally a cutting garden to supply fresh flowers for the house. Franklin Beebe was often found in this garden tending his favorite flower, the carnation. Today, the garden is planted with shade- and sun-loving perennials, from hostas to daylilies, rudbeckia, sedums, and scabiosa.

The Sunken Garden was restored in 2011 by noted landscape preservationist Lucinda Brockway. She based her design on the Beebe's original garden, but created a planting scheme that would offer more seasonal color and easier maintenance for the volunteer caretakers. The central boxwood-bordered beds bloom in shades of purple and blue in the summer with hundreds of salvias,

'Rozane' geraniums, and *verbena bonariensis*, accented with the silver foliage of artemesia, around a central feature of spiky yuccas. The outer beds feature peonies and reblooming daylilies. The focal point is a whimsical tree sculpture, "The Spirits of the Garden," by Alfred Glover, representing the passageways between the spiritual and the living in the garden.

Highfield House hosts a series of changing art exhibitions throughout the year. Beautifully curated art pieces are displayed in both the mansion and gardens.

Heritage Museums & Gardens

67 Grove St., Sandwich, MA 02563
(508) 888-3300
heritagemuseumsandgardens.org

AREA: 100 acres

HOURS: April 14–Oct. 8: daily 10–5

ADMISSION: $18

AMENITIES:

EVENTS: Rhododendron and hydrangea festivals

Heritage Museums & Gardens comprises three galleries and expansive gardens on Cape Cod. It is a destination with attractions for the whole family, from the avid gardener to children, teens, and history buffs.

The Gardens at Heritage were established by Charles Owen Dexter, a businessman who bought what was then called Shawme Farm at the age of 59 in 1921, and spent the next 20 years working there on weekends and experimenting with plant hybridizing.

His passion became rhododendrons, and he used the Chinese species *Rhododendron fortunei* to produce hybrids with dense foliage, large stature, and flowers of superior size and color, many of which were also fragrant. The popular rhododendron 'Scintillation' is one of over 160 named cultivars. More than 160 named Dexter cultivars as well as tens of thousands of unnamed plants bloom at Heritage Gardens between Memorial Day and mid-June; potted Dexter cultivars are also available for sale.

The gardens at Heritage are also particularly beautiful in July, when the hybrid daylilies, water lilies, and hydrangeas are in bloom. Heritage is home to the most comprehensive hydrangea collection in the United States, displayed in two gardens. The Cape Cod Hydrangea Society Display Garden is devoted to hybrids of the classic blue *Hydrangea macrophylla*. The North American Hydrangea Test

Garden exhibits new hybrids that will be grown and evaluated by experts from across the country.

Other areas of interest include holly, herb, hosta, and heather gardens, and more than a thousand varieties of trees, shrubs, and flowers. A labyrinth designed by Marty Cain, one of the best-known labyrinth designers in North America, provides a shaded spot for contemplation.

Children and teens will enjoy special areas designed with them in mind. Hidden Hollow is a children's outdoor discovery garden nestled in a two-acre kettle hole. Kids can climb stumps, navigate log balance beams, construct forts, dig in sand, and learn about plants in interesting ways. The new Adventure Park at Heritage combines fun and learning for children, teens, and adults, with educational forest trails and five "aerial trails" in the treetops. Tree-to-tree bridges and zip lines offer physical challenges in varying degrees of difficulty.

The galleries include a working 1908 carousel, exhibits of American arts and artifacts, American automobiles, and changing exhibits set in historic buildings.

Avant Gardens

710 High Hill Rd., Dartmouth, MA 02747
(508) 998-8819
avantgardensne.com

HOURS: Select weekends: see website

AMENITIES:

Avant Gardens has been known for over 25 years as a specialty nursery that offers rare and surprising perennials, trees, and shrubs. You will find a lilac here, but it will have golden foliage. The daphne will be only 12" high—perfect for a rock garden. The mimosa tree will have rich maroon foliage, and the bleeding heart will sport white flowers atop bright yellow leaves. Owners Katherine and Chris Tracey experiment with the unusual on the grounds of Avant Gardens, creating a home display garden that features beautiful specimen trees, flower borders, and gorgeous stonework. Chris is a master dry stone artisan, and uses traditional techniques that have been practiced for centuries in New England and the British Isles. Katherine's training as a painter and textile designer has made her a talented landscape designer with a passion for horticulture. Driven by a life motto to "grow everything at least once," she has cultivated a design aesthetic that incorporates the best uncommon plants for New England landscapes.

In the past few years, Katherine has taken a special interest in succulents, and her nursery offers dozens of varieties as well as beautifully composed succulent containers. It is also a wonderful place to find tender perennials for outstanding container combinations. The nursery is primarily mail-order, but open to the public on select weekends during the growing season.

Sylvan Nursery

1028 Horseneck Rd., Westport, MA 02790
(508) 636-4573
sylvannursery.com

HOURS: March 13–Nov 24: daily 7:30–4
AMENITIES:

Sylvan Nursery is well known in the landscape design trade. If you can't find a rare tree at a mature size, try Sylvan. If you need 100 of Hydrangea 'Unique,' try Sylvan. Heathers? Go to Sylvan. Sylvan is a nursery that caters primarily to the wholesale trade—only about 25% of the customers are garden centers, municipalities, and retail customers. What began as part-time hobby 50 years ago has grown to a booming business on 300 acres of prime land in southeastern Massachusetts, where the maritime climate assures ideal growing conditions. Plants are housed in 24 greenhouses and a huge outdoor wholesale yard that serves more than 6,000 customers in New England and the Mid-Atlantic states.

Although Sylvan does not have display gardens, the sheer volume and variety of its offerings make it worth the trip to Westport. It is best to preview their selection on the website, and come prepared with a list, comfortable shoes, a water bottle, and lots of room in the car. Children and pets should be left at home since heavy machinery will be moving about the nursery. When you arrive, check in at the office, grab a map, and plan out a route. The nursery is immense, it is easy to get lost, and the inventory is overwhelming. Sylvan has historically specialized in heaths, heathers, bearberry, and native seaside shrubs. There are about 45 varieties of heaths and heathers to peruse, as well as 75 varieties of hydrangeas, David Austen roses, and a good collection of Japanese maples in many sizes. Most of the plants are purchased bare-root and grown on-site, and half of the stock is sold balled and burlapped. The knowledgeable staff includes fourteen Massachusetts Certified Horticulturists.

Allen C. Haskell Public Gardens

787 Shawmut Ave., New Bedford, MA 02746
(508) 636-4693
thetrustees.org/places-to-visit/south-coast/haskell-public-gardens

AREA: 6 acres
HOURS: Daily dawn–dusk

Allen C. Haskell was a lifelong New Bedford resident and famed horticulturalist who ran a unique and successful nursery on this property for more than 50 years. He collected plants from all over the world and designed display gardens to teach customers how to combine plants for best effect. Over the years, Haskell won many awards at the Boston Flower Show and became a garden celebrity—visitors to the nursery included Martha Stewart, Queen Beatrix of the Netherlands, and Jacqueline Kennedy Onassis.

Haskell passed away in 2004, and the Trustees of Reservations acquired the property in 2013, opening it as the Haskell Public Gardens. It is located in the heart of New Bedford with six acres of beautifully landscaped gardens, historic buildings, and more than half an acre of greenhouse space. Like other elegant old gardens, the former nursery glows with the patina of old age. Towering trees provide shady retreats, while mossy planters, vine-draped rock walls, and dappled sunlight create an atmosphere of mystery. Mature Japanese maples, weeping hemlocks, yews, and junipers spread their majestic branches over granite cobble walkways. Thirty-foot tall Japanese umbrella pines and native big-leaf magnolias reach for the sky, while giant hostas and feathery ferns carpet the ground.

The Trustees have begun programming in the park: art exhibits, pruning classes, and wine festivals have made it into an area destination. Discovery-based family programs that encourage children to interact with the natural world are also planned.

Tranquil Lake Nursery

45 River St., Rehoboth, MA 02769
(508) 252-4002
tranquil-lake.com

AREA: 10 acres

HOURS: April 22–July 31: Wed.–Sun. 9–5; Aug. 1–Oct. 1:

Wed.–Sat. 9–5

AMENITIES:

EVENTS: Garden tours, lectures, garden workshops

Tranquil Lake Nursery is the destination of choice if you are looking for daylilies, Siberian iris, or Japanese iris. Ten acres of growing fields offer plenty of varieties. Visit in late May or June to see more than 300 varieties of Siberian Iris blooming in shades of blue, purple, pink and white. July is daylily month. Tranquil Lake Nursery is the largest grower of these plants in the Northeast, with more than 3,000 cultivars of daylilies, from the smaller reblooming varieties, to the large tetraploid hybrids. Many are introductions from New England breeders. July is also bloom time for the collection of more than 300 moisture-loving Japanese iris. You can access catalogs of the plant collections on the website, and either order online, or choose what you would like to purchase before your visit.

This daylily and iris nursery began in 1970 as a mail-order business by ardent plant collector Charles Trommer. In 1986, horticulturists Warren Leach and Philip Boucher bought the nursery and expanded the business, offering container plants as well as distinctive landscape design. Phil oversaw the daylily and iris fields, Warren managed the landscape design business, and they added display gardens. They dissolved the partnership in 2013 and the land was restricted for agricultural conservation so that it can never be developed. Warren and his wife, Debi Hogan, now run the nursery, adding a new garden or educational garden feature every year. Many of the plants in the display gardens are also available for sale.

Briggs Garden & Home

295 Kelley Blvd., North Attleboro, MA 02760
(508) 699-7421
briggsgarden.com

HOURS: Mon.–Sat. 8–6, Sun. 9–5
AMENITIES:

Briggs Garden and Home is a family-owned and operated nursery dating to 1961, when the business began as a landscape design and build company. The garden center has enjoyed a loyal following due to its excellent selection of trees and shrubs, vegetables, perennials, and annuals. In 2008 the Briggs family built a new expanded retail store, greenhouses, and nursery yard, creating a destination spot for all seasons.

The retail store is beautifully designed and staged, with a huge selection of garden necessities, ornaments and accessories. There are candles, glass balls, ceramic fish, and miniature sailboats for the beach house garden. Miniature tropicals, mosses, and elegant glass containers are displayed for the terrarium shopper. Birdhouses, from the classic copper-roofed white post top to a whimsical ceramic gourd, are available for the bird enthusiast. A charming café allows you to linger over a cappuccino or fruit smoothie and indulge in a sandwich or pastry.

The greenhouses are huge and well-stocked with tropicals, citrus trees, herbs, and baskets overflowing with gorgeous annuals. A large selection of terracotta and glazed pottery makes container gardening fun and easy. In the spring, you will find a broad selection of veggies. In the perennials area, Briggs often sells plants in a couple of different sizes, so that you can try a small plant in a 4" pot, or commit to a mature specimen in a 2-gallon pot. Perennials are displayed by color instead of Latin name, which makes selection easy for both the designer and the novice.

Briggs's large display beds feature unusual conifers, grasses, and perennials. In the nursery area, you will find an Asian garden surrounding a pond with a waterfall. Another large display bed features dwarf conifers and a rock garden surrounding a second pond. Several mixed perennial and shrub beds provide ideas for choosing companion plants.

Cochato Nursery

373 N. Franklin St., Holbrook, MA 02343
(781) 767-9770
cochatonursery.com

HOURS: Mid April–Labor Day: Thurs. 10–3, Fri.–Sat. 9–5, Sun. 9–4 & by appointment

AMENITIES:

Cochato Nursery is a wonderful source for hosta, shade plants, and unusual specimens. Owners Chuck Doughty and Sue DuBrava founded the nursery 25 years ago as a source of unusual plants for their landscape design business. They opened the nursery on their property and planted award-winning display gardens to showcase their unique selections. The Doughtys are welcoming and extremely knowledgeable about all aspects of the plant world. They are generous with their time and will be happy to advise.

The Doughtys are hosta collectors and active members of hosta societies. Cochato offers about 600 hosta varieties at any one time, along with an impressive selection of companion plants—ferns, woodland wildflowers, and shade perennials. There are trilliums, uvularia, hellebores, woodland peonies, and other shade lovers that you will not find at most nurseries, along with rare trees and water garden plants. The inventory may not be large, but the selectivity is excellent.

The display gardens at Cochato are framed by an immense hardscape, starting with native boulders that were left behind from the Ice Age. The Doughtys have added granite stone bridges, antique gristmill grinding wheels, Staddle stones, stone troughs, and fountains. Cochato means "running water" in the Native American Algonquin dialect, and the gardens display three koi ponds—with running streams, waterfalls, and giant fish—encircled by bog gardens planted with pitcher plants. A scree garden delights rock garden enthusiasts, and a garden railway is popular with children and adults alike. Mature dwarf conifers, spring ephemerals, rare native plants, and unusual cultivars create a goldmine for plant geeks and collectors.

Eleanor Cabot Bradley Estate

2468B Washington St. (Route 138), Canton, MA 02021
(781) 784-0567
thetrustees.org/places-to-visit/greater-boston/bradley-estate.html

AREA: 90 acres

HOURS: Gardens: daily dawn–dusk

ADMISSION: Gardens free

AMENITIES:

EVENTS: Tours of house and gardens

A visit to the Eleanor Cabot Bradley Estate will transport you back 100 years to gracious, turn-of-the-century living in the Neponset River Valley. Though located just a short distance from busy Rte. 128, this 90-acre historic estate features an elegant house, formal and kitchen gardens, fields and woodlands, and a small working farm.

Eleanor Cabot Bradley inherited the estate in 1945 from her uncle, Arthur Tracy Cabot. Dr. Cabot had hired Charles Platt to design the gardens. Platt was renowned for infusing American gardens with the classical Italian aesthetic. The Italianate walled parterre garden at the rear of the mansion was the centerpiece of the Cabot garden. Platt designed the four-foot-tall red brick lattice wall with its open filigree design to add filtered light, enclosure, structure, and ornament to the garden. Within the enclosed space is Italian formality: clipped box

hedges, a wide-open lawn outlined with a gravel walkway, symmetrical flower beds, and a classical fountain.

Platt's design included a manicured lawn extending beyond the brick pillars to a view of the hills of the Neponset River Valley. The restrained formality of the enclosed garden was contrasted by informal plantings of rhododendron, azalea, and dogwood in the outlying landscape. A rhododendron walk led from the enclosed garden through the woods to the kitchen garden.

Eleanor Bradley was an avid gardener, and studied landscape design at Radcliffe, the Arnold Arboretum, and the Massachusetts Horticultural Society. The Bradleys preserved the formal gardens and original plantings, and added ponds, specimen trees, a sunken camellia garden, and an art studio. Eleanor was a friend and benefactor of the Arnold Arboretum, and in 1985 the Arboretum created the Eleanor Cabot Bradley Rosaceous Collection in her honor, and included roses from her garden in the collection. She left her estate to the Trustees of Reservations in 1991, and thanks to her foresight this beautiful property is protected in perpetuity.

In 2017 horticulture director Jeff Thompson and the Trustees formed a unique partnership with Proven Winners and created a brand-new display garden of shrubs, perennials, and showy annuals. The theme was Violet Riot, and it featured a provocative color combination of chartreuse and purple. The formal beds and urns were planted with papyrus, heliotrope, salvia, purple elephant ears, 'Royal Velvet' Supertunias, 'Black Lace' elderberry, 'Fishnet Stockings' coleus, and brand-new varieties of sweet-potato vines called 'Green with Envy' and 'After Midnight.' The effect was a stunning revitalization of a classical garden, packed with wonderful plant combinations ideas for gardeners.

Arnold Arboretum

125 Arborway, Boston, MA 02130
617-524-1718
arboretum.harvard.edu

AREA: 281 acres

HOURS: Daily sunrise–sunset

ADMISSION: Free, donations appreciated

AMENITIES:

EVENTS: Guided tours, classes, lectures, Lilac Sunday

The Arnold Arboretum is one of the premier horticultural institutions in the United States. An allied institution of Harvard University, the Arboretum holds 14,760 different plants representing 3,800 botanical and horticultural taxa, with particular emphasis on the woody species of North America and eastern Asia. Important collections include beech, honeysuckle, magnolia, crabapple, oak, rhododendron, and lilac.

The Arboretum was created thanks to the generosity of New Bedford whaling merchant James Arnold, who directed $100,000 of his estate to Harvard College for the establishment of an arboretum. Charles Sprague Sargent was appointed the Arboretum's first director in 1873 and spent the following 54 years shaping it into a world-class collection and research facility.

In a creative lease agreement forged between the City of Boston and Harvard in 1882, the Arnold Arboretum became part of the city park system, but the Arboretum staff retained control of the collections. As a result the Arboretum became part of the famous Emerald Necklace system of parks designed by Frederick Law Olmstead. Sargent and Olmstead collaborated on the layout of the Arboretum's path, roads, and planting areas. Sargent decided to arrange the plant collections by family and genus, and Olmstead took advantage of the natural contours of the land and designed gently curving paths that would give close access to the collections.

You can visit the Arboretum any time of year. Bloom starts in March with witch hazel and willows, followed in April by forsythias and small-leaved rhododendrons. The spring season is ablaze with magnolias, shadbush, crabapple, quince, enkianthus, viburnums, weigelas, and silverbells. Of all the plants in the Arboretum, only one, the lilac, is granted its own daylong celebration every year. With over 165 different lilac hybrids, the lilac collection at the Arboretum is one of the best in the United States. Lilac Sunday is typically in mid-May, with garden tours, family activities, and food vendors.

During June roses, mock oranges, rhododendrons, and mountain laurels provide color and fragrance. In July and August, the hydrangeas, stewartias, clethra, aralias, and pagoda trees bloom. Buddleias attract butterflies and hummingbirds in September. Autumn is a gorgeous time with deciduous trees—particularly the maples—putting on a spectacular show. In winter, the conifer collection is a must-see. A bonsai collection of 35 masterful specimens boasts six hinoki cypress that are between 150 and 275 years old.

Sargent also established the Arnold Arboretum as a leading scientific institution. He developed a comprehensive library devoted to botany, horticulture, and trees, and an equally notable herbarium of woody plant specimens from around the world. The Arboretum's involvement in global botanical and horticultural exploration, especially in eastern Asia, greatly expanded our knowledge of many

new plants and brought them into cultivation.

Today, the Arboretum is launching a new era of discovery, focused on collecting exceptional representatives of botanical variation from the Northern Hemisphere. The agenda is spurred by widespread destruction of native plant habitats due to global development, as well as threats to plant diversity caused by rapid climate change. Announced in 2016, the plan calls for 10 years of global exploration to collect as many samples as possible of woody plants that will grow in Boston's temperate but warming climate. Sargeant would be proud.

Rose Kennedy Greenway

Boston, MA
(617) 292-0020
rosekennedygreenway.org

AREA: 6 Sets of Parks: North End, Wharf District, Fort Point Channel, Dewey Square, Chinatown, Armenian Heritage
HOURS: Daily 7–11
ADMISSION: Free
EVENTS: Group horticulture tours, changing special programs

The Rose Kennedy Greenway is a mile-and-a-half of contemporary parks in the heart of Boston. It connects people and the city with horticulture, beauty, and fun. It is situated on the site of what was once an elevated highway that separated the historic waterfront from downtown Boston. The Greenway was inaugurated in late 2008 and encompasses gardens, tree-lined promenades, historic landmarks, plazas, fountains, carousel, public art, food vendors and entertainment. Its stewardship is in the hands of the Greenway Conservancy, which maintains the parks and partners with cultural institutions to create a vibrant selection of programs.

Each set of parks within the Greenway—North End, Wharf District, Fort Point Channel, Dewey Square, Chinatown and Armenian Heritage—was designed to complement the character of its Bos-

ton neighborhood. The North End Parks feature a long pergola overlooking a reflecting pool with fountains that serves as the "front porch" to this historic neighborhood. Several flowering trees, including yellow 'Elizabeth' magnolias, encircle the gardens. Lush plantings of daffodils, roses, Russian sage, lavender, purple cone flower, iris, and daylilies are enclosed by boxwood hedges to evoke the formal style of historic European gardens.

Adjacent to Faneuil Hall, the Armenian Heritage Park commemorates Boston as a port of entry for immigrants. At its heart is a modern split-dodecahedron sculpture in a reflecting pool, which represents the immigrant experience. The two halves are reconfigured annually to symbolize all who left their country of origin and found a new life in America. The accompanying Labyrinth celebrates life's journey. The single jet of water and eternity symbol at its center represent hope and rebirth.

The Wharf District Parks connect Faneuil Hall and the Financial District with the Boston Harbor. Wide public spaces, tree-lined walkways, and benches allow you to enjoy a range of plants native to New England and the Northeast. The Mother's Walk is a winding path inscribed by sons and daughters with the names of the special people that have loved and cared for them.

The Fort Point Channel Parks, between Oliver and Congress streets and Atlantic Avenue, feature colorful plantings that enclose a lawn designed for relaxing. Yoshino cherries and native serviceberries are harbingers of early spring, while tree peonies wow visitors in May, and 'Lady in Red' hydrangeas captivate in July.

Dewey Square Park, located between Congress and Summer streets and Atlantic Avenue, has Demonstration Gardens that illustrate sustainable gardening practices for urban gardeners. The garden is planted with pollinator plants to attract

beneficial insects, unusual edibles, and Northeast natives that are suitable for rain gardens.

Entered by a huge modern red gate, the China-town Park is an oasis at the southern end of the Greenway, which draws upon Asian traditions and artwork. A walkway edged by bamboo and bright red sculptural elements winds past a long fountain resembling a shallow riverbed with waterfalls. The gardens display Asian plants. Rhododendrons, cherry trees, irises, peonies, and chrysanthemums provide seasonal color, while grasses, bamboo, Chinese elms, and Pagoda trees provide texture and structure year-round.

The Greenway is Boston's only organically-main-tained public park. The Greenway Conservancy is committed to organic and sustainable landscape management. As a result, plants are healthy and resilient—better able to withstand the wear of public use—and children and pets can safely play on the lawns.

Longfellow House

105 Brattle St., Cambridge, MA 02138
(617) 876-4491
www.nps.gov/long/index.htm

AREA: 2 acres

HOURS: Gardens: daily dawn-dusk; house: May 24–Oct. 29, Wed.–Sun. 9:30–5

ADMISSION: Gardens, free

AMENITIES:

EVENTS: Annual plant sale in May

A National Historic Site, Longfellow House served as General George Washington's headquarters for nine months during the Siege of Boston. It later became the home of 19th century poet Henry W. Longfellow and stayed in the Longfellow family for more than 100 years. It's a place to explore American history, literature, and arts, and to enjoy a 19th century garden.

Henry Wadsworth Longfellow occupied the house from 1837 to 1882. As a professor of languages at Harvard College, he first rented rooms in the house. When he married Frances Appleton in 1843, her wealthy father bought the house for them as a wedding present. Painted a proper yellow with white trim and black shutters, the late-Georgian mansion radiated affluence, dignity, and tradition. A wonderful meadow sloped down from the house to the Charles River, creating a bit of country in a busy city.

During his years as a boarder, Longfellow developed a keen interest in the grounds. Shortly after his wedding, he installed a lyre-shaped garden, and created allées lined with trees imported from Europe and the West Coast. When the lyre shape proved impractical, he hired landscape architect Richard Dolben to create a new design in 1847. The resulting garden was a square surrounding a circle that was cut into four tear-shaped garden beds outlined by trimmed boxwood, which Frances referred to as a "Persian rug."

After Longfellow's death, the nine-acre property was divided among his children, who built houses on their plots. The oldest daughter, Alice, became the home's caretaker and hired Martha Brookes Hutcheson to restore the garden. Hutcheson's design was very much in the Colonial Revival style, with a central boxwood parterre garden, brick walkways, chinoiserie fencing, and a large pergola. Twenty years after the garden was installed, Ellen Biddle Shipman created a new planting design with heirloom roses, evergreen and ornamental trees that added height, and towering delphiniums, phlox, and hollyhocks that gave the garden a billowy style. In 1913 Alice established the Longfellow House Trust to preserve the house and grounds.

In 2000, the National Park Service and the Friends of the Longfellow House began to restore the gardens as they were in Alice Longfellow's day. At the front of the house, new elms were planted, the walkway widened, and roses planted to climb the façade of the house as they did a century ago. The gardens were renewed with old-fashioned roses, Canterbury bells, dahlias, lilies, foxgloves, peonies, iris, poppies, and dozens of other perennials, annuals, and bulbs to provide blooms throughout the seasons

"In all places, then, and in all seasons,
Flowers expand their light and soul-like wings,
Teaching us, by most persuasive reasons,
How akin they are to human things."

"Flowers" by Henry Wadsworth Longfellow (1837)

Mount Auburn Cemetery

580 Mount Auburn St., Cambridge, MA 02138
(617) 547-7105
mountauburn.org

AREA: 175 acres
HOURS: Daily 8–7
ADMISSION: Free

Located four miles outside of Boston, Mount Auburn was America's first designed rural cemetery. It also gave rise to the American park movement and became an eminent horticultural institution.

In the early 19th century, Dr. Jacob Bigelow, a Boston physician and Harvard professor, became concerned that crowded cemeteries in congested urban areas might promote the spread of contagious diseases. At that time, most city residents were buried in churchyards or vaults below churches, and as the population of Boston grew, these options became untenable. Dr. Bigelow developed the vision of a burial place located on the outskirts of the city, with family burial lots sited in a landscaped setting filled with trees, shrubs, and flowers. In 1831, the newly formed Massachusetts Horticultural Society agreed to take a lead role in developing the first rural cemetery. They found a 72-acre farm in Watertown and Cambridge that was ideal and featured a 125-foot central mount that provided spectacular views of Boston and Cambridge.

Henry A.S. Dearborn, President of the Massachusetts Horticultural Society, was largely responsible for the cemetery's design. He incorporated ideas from the English Picturesque Landscape style and the Père Lachaise Cemetery in Paris into his plan for Mount Auburn. The Picturesque style celebrated nature and embraced the topography and unique physical characteristics of a site. It also incorporated architectural elements such as castles, rustic cottages, and Gothic ruins into its design, which was particularly suited to a cemetery with its statuary and mausoleums. Dearborn partnered with civil engineer Alexander Wardworth in laying out winding roads that followed the natural contours of the land, and retaining naturalistic elements such as wooded areas and ponds. He also established a separate experimental garden at Mount Auburn, planted with many domestic and exotic varieties of fruits, flowers, and vegetables. As news of the garden cemetery spread, horticulturalists from around the world sent gifts of seeds.

The popularity of the new cemetery grew, and lots sold quickly. It was open to all races and religions, and became a popular choice for Boston's African Americans in the 19th century. It also became the final resting place for such prominent Bostonians as Mary Baker Eddy, Isabella Stewart Gardner, Winslow Homer, and Henry Wadsworth Longfellow. In 1835 the cemetery became a private nonprofit corporation, ended its partnership with the Massachusetts Horticultural Society, and the experimental garden was discontinued.

By the mid-1800s, the site was internationally renowned as a horticultural attraction and pleasure ground, with picturesque landscapes, winding paths, a variety of horticulture, and sculptural art. Its success inspired the designs of other cemeteries, and launched the American parks movement. Today, the cemetery still upholds Bigelow's natural, oasis-like vision, and contains more than 5,000 trees spanning 600 varieties. They include Japanese umbrella pines, yellowwoods, amur cork trees, plane trees, weeping cherries, sweetgum, and weeping pagoda trees. Mount Auburn has become a world-renowned ornamental horticultural landscape, a National Historic Landmark, and a leader in historic landscape preservation and ecologically sustainable landscaping. It continues to function as an active cemetery and a pastoral landscape that is visited each year by more than 200,000 people from around the world.

Lyman Estate

185 Lyman St., Waltham, MA 02452
(617) 994-6672
historicnewengland.org/property/lyman-estate/

AREA: 37 acres

HOURS: Gardens & greenhouses: daily dawn–dusk; mansion: third Sat. 10–1

ADMISSION: Gardens: free; mansion: $8

AMENITIES: 🚻 👫 ♿

EVENTS: 5 specialty plant sales, camellia viewing

The Lyman Estate was built in 1793 by Boston shipping merchant Theodore Lyman and was the family's summer residence for 150 years. It consisted of a 24-room Federal style mansion set on 400 acres of woodlands, lawns, gardens, greenhouses, a deer park, and a working farm. The mansion and its 37 acres of gardens and greenhouses have been preserved by Historic New England and are open for touring.

Called The Vale because of its low-lying situation alongside a stream, the Lyman Estate is a rare example of late 18th century garden design. Fashioned after English country estates, it was de-

signed by British landscape designer William Bell with rolling pastures, wide lawns, winding paths, and ponds that are characteristic of the Picturesque style. Scenic vistas were framed by groups of trees, while functional areas like the kitchen and cutting gardens were screened from view. Warmed by the sun, a 600-foot-long south-facing brick wall behind the house was used for espaliering tender peach trees. Lyman imported some of the first European copper beeches to America, and one of these still stands beside the Camellia House. The sugar maples lining the entrance road and the large tulip tree by the parking lot are also original, but many of the estate's old trees were downed by the 1938 hurricane.

The family embellished the landscape with flower gardens and flowering shrubs in the late 1800s. Rhododendrons, flame and pink-shell azaleas, and magnolias planted before the Civil War continue to bloom each spring. The landscape is in the process of restoration to its 1920s appearance.

The main features of the property are the estate's four greenhouses, which are among the oldest surviving greenhouses in the U.S. The Grape House was originally built in 1804 to raise exotic fruits such as oranges, pineapples, and bananas. It now houses Green Muscat grapevines and Black Hamburg grapes grown from cuttings taken in 1870 from the Royal Greenhouses at Hampton Court in England. The Camellia House was built circa 1820 for the cultivation of these beautiful trees imported from China, Japan, and Korea. Camellia cultivation was a popular pursuit among Boston's gentry, and many of the Lyman camellias are more than 100 years old. The Orchid House exhibits rare orchids that are covered with blooms throughout the year. The Sales Greenhouse offers unusual houseplants, citrus trees, camellias, orchids, and herbs, as well as gardening supplies and gifts.

Ropes Mansion

318 Essex St., Salem, MA 01970
(978) 745-9500
pem.org

AREA: 3 acres

HOURS: Gardens: daily dawn–dusk; mansion: Sat.–Sun. 12–4

ADMISSION: Free

AMENITIES:

Like many places in Salem, the Ropes Mansion comes with its own ghost story. Built in the 1720s by merchant Samuel Barnard, the mansion was purchased by Judge Nathaniel Ropes II in 1768. An unpopular Loyalist judge, Ropes died of small-pox while his house was being stoned by an angry mob in 1774. The family went into exile during the Revolutionary War but reclaimed their home after the war ended. In 1839, Ropes's widow, Abigail, died after her dress caught fire from the fireplace. Both are said to haunt the mansion.

The Ropes family inhabited the house until 1907, when it was converted to the Ropes Memorial. To-day it is owned and operated by the Peabody Essex Museum. The mansion was reopened in 2015 after a six-year restoration, and the museum used the family's extensive records to guide the process.

Filled with original furnishings, the house con-tains superb examples of 18th and 19th century furniture, ceramics, glass, silver, and textiles. The rooms have been artfully staged to offer glimpses into the family's life: tables are set for meals, and bedrooms are scattered with personal items.

Behind the austere white Colonial Revival man-sion, the garden is a hidden jewel. It was designed by John Robinson in 1912 in a formal style and is sheltered by a classical Italian brick wall. As you enter through the first arbor, you will find a small running brook, which leads to a cool, shaded pool stocked with koi, complete with overhanging flowers and lily pads. The pond was added in 1931. There are benches throughout the garden, and you can admire several original plantings, including the wisteria arbor and the large copper beech.

The main garden has a symmetrical layout around a circular central bed anchored by a sundial. A full-time gardener maintains the impeccable grounds and grows an astounding array of colorful annuals, dahlias, lilies, roses, hydrangeas, and perennials.

Sedgwick Gardens at Long Hill

572 Essex St., Beverly, MA 01915
(978) 921-1944
thetrustees.org/places-to-visit/north-shore/long-hill.html

AREA: 114 acres

HOURS: Garden: daily 8–5

ADMISSION: Gardens free

AMENITIES:

EVENTS: Annual plant sale in May, guided tours

In 1916, Ellery Sedgwick, editor and publisher of *Atlantic Monthly*, and his wife, Mabel Cabot Sedgwick, selected this property as a summer retreat. They built an elegant Federal style house they called Long Hill—a replica of Isaac Ball's plantation in Charleston, South Carolina. When the Ball house was set to be demolished, the Sedgwicks purchased and reused the original elegant woodwork and mantles in their own house. Bricks from an old Ipswich mill were incorporated into the walls of Long Hill, giving it the look of a much older home. In designing the interior, the couple evoked the outdoors with lovely murals of garden scenes and flowers.

Mabel Cabot Sedgwick, an accomplished gardener, horticulturist, and author of *The Garden Month by Month* published in 1907, set about designing gardens and landscape amenities that are renowned a century later. After her death in 1937, her vision was expanded by the second

Mrs. Sedgwick, the former Marjorie Russell, a rare-plants specialist who added new species of trees and shrubs to the estate, some of which were introduced by the Arnold Arboretum.

The six acres of gardens around the mansion are arranged as formal, geometric outdoor rooms. Each room is distinct in its own way, accented by ornaments and statuary. The gardens mainly occupy the south-facing slope, which allowed plants like Davidia (handkerchief tree) and Southern magnolia to grow this far north.

Close to the house, white ironwork pavilions and metal arches supporting clematis adorn the gardens and create the distinctive look of Long Hill. Formal balustrades and fan-shaped steps add subtle hints of formality. A hosta-lined path leads from the white arches to a lotus pool. The Horseshoe Garden features statuary along with a small wooden Chinese pagoda, which had been a wellhead from a Beverly farm in a previous life. Other gardens feature a rose arbor, croquet lawn, and small pools inhabited by frogs and fish. Weeping hemlocks, arborvitae hedges, cherry trees, and Japanese tree peonies separate one view from the next. Collections of natives such as blueberries, magnolias, and eastern red cedar are punctuated with Asian imports such as Japanese wisteria, stewartia, kousa dogwood, Regel's three-wing nut, and witchhazel. Long Hill is a delight for plant collectors as well as garden design buffs.

The gardens are surrounded on all sides by more than 100 acres of apple orchards, meadows, and woodland with a 1.2-mile loop trail. The Sedgwicks grew vegetables and raised horses, cows and chickens. These farming traditions are continued on the property with a 2-acre organic vegetable farm with chickens. A small but densely planted children's garden is a fun, manageable place for kids to dig and explore.

Crane Estate

290 Argilla Rd., Ipswich, MA 01938
(978) 356-4351
thetrustees.org/crane-estate/

AREA: 165 acres

HOURS: Gardens: Tues.–Sun. dawn–dusk; mansion: 10–4

ADMISSION: $10 per car

AMENITIES:

EVENTS: Landscape tours: Thurs. & Sun. 3 pm.

The spectacular Crane Estate encompasses more than 2,100 acres overlooking Ipswich Bay on the North Shore of Massachusetts. The Estate comprises three properties: Castle Hill, which is a National Historic Landmark mansion with gardens; Crane Beach, which is a spectacular public beach; and the Crane Wildlife Refuge, a natural treasure boasting many rare plant and animal species.

Chicago industrialist Richard T. Crane, Jr., and his wife, Florence, first purchased the property in 1910. Captivated by the beauty of the landscape, he worked with eight leading architects and landscape architects to shape his summer retreat. In 1928, Crane crowned the estate with a grand 59-room, Stuart-style mansion, designed by world-renowned architect David Adler. A pair of Art Deco griffins given to Crane by his employees upon completion of his new house, graced the entrance to the north terrace overlooking the sea.

During its heyday the estate was quite self-sufficient. The Cranes raised livestock and maintained root cellars, vegetable gardens, and orchards with the help of 60 or so gardeners. An on-site 134,000-gallon underground cistern supplied water (it's now back in use), and a coal-fired power plant supplied electricity.

Although the mansion was formal in style, the estate was designed for fun and entertaining. For eight idyllic weeks each summer, the Cranes enjoyed their paradise with lavish picnics, parties, and boat trips. The property included a maze, a log cabin playhouse, a bowling green, tennis court, billiard room, walking paths, deer park, golf course, and the sand beach.

Castle Hill's formal gardens recently have been restored to their original beauty. The Italian Garden, designed by the Olmstead Brothers, was Florence Crane's favorite. This hidden oasis features colorful perennial beds enclosed by walls and terraces. Two octagonal teahouses are linked by a pergola on one end, and a columned balcony above a fountain and pool encloses the other end.

The sunken Rose Garden has yet to be restored. It lies across the road from the Italian Garden, and contained four beds of roses around a central pool with fountain. Stucco columns supported a wooden pergola, and hundreds of shrub and climbing roses flowered there.

In 1915 Arthur Shurcliff added the Grand Allée, a half-mile long, 160-foot wide stretch of lawn, bordered by two rows of evergreens and classical statuary. An Italianate "Casino Complex" tucked into the allée's first hillside had a courtyard with a saltwater swimming pool that was bookended by two villas: one housing a ballroom, the other providing "bachelors' quarters" for the young men who visited. In Italian gardens, the "casino" simply meant "small house" and was often the name for

the summer house. The Casino Complex was restored in 2016, and now offers a trimmed lawn for croquet (the pool had been filled in long before), and a new brick terrace with marble statues and comfortable chairs and tables. The former ballroom now holds a café, along with a billiards table and entertainment for children. The Grand Allée was restored in 2012, with 700 trees planted to replace old and storm-damaged ones.

Sadly, Richard Crane died of a heart attack in 1931, so he enjoyed his house for a very short time. In 1945, the family gave 1,000 acres of beach and dunes to The Trustees of Reservations in his memory. Florence Crane continued to spend summers at Castle Hill until her death in 1949. She bequeathed an additional 350 acres and the mansion to The Trustees, who maintain it to this day. Within the last 15 years, about $6 million has been invested in capital improvements. Two granddaughters reside in Ipswich and remain involved with the property.

Stevens-Coolidge Place

137 Andover St., North Andover, MA 01845
(978) 682-3580
thetrustees.org/places-to-visit/north-shore/stevens-coolidge-place.html

AREA: 91 acres

HOURS: Gardens: daily dawn–dusk

ADMISSION: Free

EVENTS: House tours, yoga in the garden, painting in the garden, family workshops and programs

The Stevens-Coolidge Place is a prime example of a Country Place estate—a style that was popular with wealthy Americans in the early part of the 20th century. The Stevenses were one of the founding families of North Andover, farming at what was originally called Ashdale Farm since 1729. In 1914 Helen Stevens inherited the estate, and with her husband, John Gardner Coolidge, transformed the farm into an elegant summer residence.

John Coolidge was member of the Boston elite—the nephew of Isabella Stewart Gardner and a descendant of Thomas Jefferson. The Coolidges hired preservation architect Joseph Everett Chandler to remodel the house and garden in the Colonial Revival style that swept the country after the 1876 Centennial Exhibition in Philadelphia.

Chandler's design for the exterior was based on a formal layout of garden rooms with informal plantings. The main gardens were sited behind the house to offer privacy. The house opened onto a shaded brick terrace that offered views of the perennial garden, which was enclosed by hedges and laid out in a pattern of rectilinear beds with colorful perennials. The Italian-style fragrant Rose Garden replaced the old barn, cow yard, and pig sty. Adjacent to the perennial garden, the Rose Garden could also be entered through an upper terrace, which provided a wonderful view of the flowers. The neighboring greenhouse complex allowed for a grapery, potted tropicals for the house, and plant propagation.

The Coolidges became enamored with chateau gardens while they lived in France during WWI, and Chandler designed for them a French flower garden, screened on one side by a brick Serpentine Wall. Modeled after those designed by Thomas Jefferson for the University of Virginia, the wall supports espaliered fruit trees. The garden was eventually converted to lawn, but in 2000 the original layout was restored and replanted with an incredible display of annuals, herbs, and vegetables.

Ashdale Farm maintained its agricultural heritage throughout Helen Stevens Coolidge's lifetime. The family kept farm animals, grew vegetables in the kitchen garden, and harvested apples from their orchard. When Helen Stevens Coolidge died in 1962, she left the property and an endowment to The Trustees of Reservations. Many of her gardens have been restored to their former appearance. The surrounding fields and woodlands provide a natural habitat for wildlife.

The Gardens at Elm Bank

900 Washington St., Wellesley, MA 02482
(617) 933-4900
masshort.org

AREA: 36 acres

HOURS: May 1–Oct 12: Tues.–Sun. 10–4

ADMISSION: $10

AMENITIES:

EVENTS: Lectures & classes, Gardener's Fair, Festival of Trees

The last private owners of the Elm Bank estate were Alice Cheney Baltzell and her husband Dr. William Baltzell. She inherited the property from her parents, who were both ardent gardeners. Her father, Benjamin Pierce Cheney, was a wealthy businessman, a member of the Massachusetts Horticultural Society and one of its most generous supporters. Alice and William Baltzell built the impressive neo-Georgian 40-room manor house in 1907. They had grand visions for the property, and employed the firm of Olmstead and Vaux to create a pleasure garden for entertaining. The original gardens included the Italianate Garden, a brick patio with an arched wrought iron gate, and a watery inlet with a Japanese bridge, an Asian Garden, and a boathouse.

Since 2001, Elm Bank has served as the headquarters of the Massachusetts Horticultural Society.

The Society has restored and expanded some of the original gardens to include educational and recreational areas for children and adults. The Italianate Garden with its 16-foot-tall purple beech hedge was restored to its original beauty. Symmetrical beds and paths lead to a central lily pond with a 14th-century baptismal font that the Baltzells purchased in Italy on their honeymoon. The surrounding beds are planted with stunning combinations of annuals. Guarding the entrance to the Italianate Garden are the three goddesses of horticulture: Flora, Ceres, and Pomona. Originally these statues graced Horticultural Hall in Boston.

Closest to the entry at Elm Bank is the New England Trial Garden. This garden is used to test and display the newest and best varieties of annuals submitted for evaluation by commercial plant breeders. Some of these new varieties are then nominated for the All-America Selections awards.

Next to the Trial Garden is the whimsical Weezie's Children's Garden, designed by Julie Moir Messervy. The space comprises a series of small spiraling gardens, each with its own theme and unique way of engaging the senses. In the center lies Tortoise Island with water play activities, surrounded by slabs of petrified wood and a spray fountain. A Raked Sand garden is usually populated with dump trucks and buckets, and the Mount with its viewing tower allows children to climb and look over the garden from on high. A miniature vegetable garden illustrates where food comes from. Other areas include the Maypole Garden, a Bamboo Garden, a Bluebird Garden complete with oversized birds' nests, and a Butterfly Garden with towering perennials in late summer.

The Bressingham Garden, designed by renowned nurseryman Adrian Bloom, is magnificent in all seasons. Large island beds display sublime combinations of perennials, grasses, trees, and shrubs. A river-like swath of Geranium 'Rozanne'

runs through the garden. Serpentine grass paths encourage strolling and seeing the gardens from many perspectives. Now 10 years old, the garden has matured to a grand display.

Additional sections of Elm Bank include The Garden to Table Vegetable Garden, the Jim Crockett Memorial Garden, and the Noanet Garden Club Historic Daffodil Garden, as well as display gardens of the Daylily Society, Rhododendron Society, and New England Herb Society.

Garden in the Woods

180 Hemenway Rd., Framingham, MA 01701
508-877-7630
newfs.org/visit/Garden-in-the-Woods

AREA: 45 acres

HOURS: April 15–Oct. 31: daily 10–5

ADMISSION: $12

AMENITIES: 🚻 🏛 ♿   Boxed lunches can be ordered

EVENTS: New audio tour, guided tours, classes, lectures

Garden in the Woods is a living museum of rare and common native plants set on 45 acres. It is also the home of the New England Wild Flower Society, whose mission is to conserve and promote the region's native plants, and encourage both home and professional gardeners to choose natives when they plant outdoor spaces.

Garden in the Woods began in 1931 when Will C. Curtis, a self-trained botanist and landscape architecture graduate of Cornell University, purchased 30 acres in north Framingham. He began clearing, planting, and sharing his garden with others. When he opened the garden to the public in 1934, Curtis wrote: "I am bringing together all the Wild Flowers and Ferns hardy in this latitude and establishing them in natural environments where they can easily be reached and enjoyed by the interested public."

As he entered his 80s, Curtis became concerned about the future of his garden in the midst of a busy city. In an agreement with the New England Wild Flower Society, he pledged to donate the garden if an endowment of $250,000 could be raised. Wild flower hobbyists from every state and Canada, along with 450 different garden clubs, conservation groups, foundations and businesses, heeded the call. On Curtis's 82nd birthday in 1965, the deed was transferred to the Society. With the land came Curtis' collection of nearly 2,000 native plant species. Within a few years, the Society moved from its Boston headquarters to the garden, added a nature center, and purchased 15 acres of adjoining land as a buffer from surrounding housing developments.

Today the Garden is the largest landscaped collection of wildflowers in New England, containing over 1,700 kinds of plants representing about 1,000 species, 200 of which rare and endangered. Ponds fringed by native blue irises, swamps with skunk cabbage, and a bog where carnivorous yellow pitcher plants catch flies illustrate the variety of Massachusetts habitats. Rare and common native flora create a changing tapestry of flowers and foliage throughout the seasons. The best time to visit Garden in the Woods is in the spring, when the blooms of trout lilies, squirrel corn, Virginia bluebells, pink lady's slipper orchids, Canada violets, blue woodland phlox, twinleaf, and Jack-in-the-pulpits cover the forest floor. In late spring, rhododendrons and azaleas burst into bloom, followed by clethra and the legendary franklinia in summer. Curtis was a fan of white flowers, and you see them everywhere: white varieties of wild geranium, bluebells, Virginia rose, great lobelia and cardinal flower. Partridgeberry and red baneberry, which normally produce red fruit, here produce white.

Since the gardens are planted with natives and

maintained organically, they attract a multitude of butterflies, honeybees, and other insect pollinators, as well as frogs, turtles, black snakes, dragonflies, and birds.

Although the plantings look spontaneous, most of the plants were raised from seeds cultivated at the Society's Nasami Farm nursery and meticulously placed in the landscape. A wide selection of native plants is available for sale at the gift shop. You can also purchase plants at Nasami Farm from April to early October; Saturday and Sundays, 10-5, and weekdays by appointment. 128 North St., Whately, MA, (413) 397-9922

Weston Nurseries

93 E. Main St., Hopkinton, MA 01748
(508) 435-3414
westonnurseries.com

HOURS: Daily 9-5; call for winter hours

AMENITIES:

EVENTS: Workshops on fairy gardens, tufa troughs, seed starting, holiday wreaths and more. Second location at 160 Pine Hill Rd., Chelmsford, MA

Most commercial nurseries purchase plants from large growers, but a small number propagate and grow their own stock. Weston Nurseries is unique in that it has been hybridizing and introducing new shrub varieties suited to the New England climate for almost 80 years.

Weston Nurseries was founded by Peter Mezitt, a Latvian immigrant who fled conscription into the Russian army in the early 1900s. As a gardener, he worked his way across Europe until he saved enough money to sail to America in 1911. Settling in Massachusetts, Mezitt continued to work as an estate gardener and greenhouse night watchman while pursuing a degree from the University of Massachusetts, Amherst. With his wife, Olga, he launched a horticultural business rooting under-stock and grafting fruit trees for local orchards.

The business grew, and in 1923 the Mezitts pur-

chased 80 acres in Weston, where they founded Weston Nurseries. By the early 1940s they had 200 acres of full-scale production facility and began breeding rhododendrons. Their son Ed introduced the hardy violet 'PJM' rhododendron and named it in honor of his father. The PJM is widely acclaimed as one of the most beautiful and resilient rhododendrons, and is probably the most widely planted rhododendron in the United States. Other introductions followed, including the pure white 'Molly Fordham,' the pink 'Olga Mezitt' and 'Weston's Aglo,' and the red-purple 'Midnight Ruby.'

By 1950 Weston Nurseries had expanded and moved to rural Hopkinton. The Mezitts' goal was to develop plants that were hardy to Zone 5 in New England, possessed a compact habit and su-perior foliage, were pest and disease resistant, and had a long blooming season. They focused their hybridizing efforts on small and large-leaf rhodo-dendrons, evergreen azaleas, and summer-flower-ing deciduous azaleas. The new introductions were rigorously tested in tough growing conditions—rocky, clay soil, full sun, and exposed hillsides—ensuring that they would do well in gardens with better growing conditions.

Some of the best known Weston introductions are the gorgeous 'Henry's Red,' which offers one of the deepest colors to be found in large-leaf rhododen-drons; and the evergreen azaleas 'Bixby,' with dark red flowers, the bright pink 'Pink Clusters,' and purple 'Royal Pillow.' Their many summer-bloom-ing deciduous azaleas offer hardiness, fragrance, and a rainbow of colors from pale yellows to golds, oranges, pinks, and reds.

In addition to their own hybrids, Weston offers a large selection of trees, shrubs, perennials, and annuals; several greenhouses with tender plants;

pottery and statuary; landscape pavers and natural stone; and a well-stocked gift shop. Display gardens include a railway garden, a pond garden, and a drought-tolerant patio garden. In the winter the nursery sells Christmas trees and hand-decorated wreaths, planters and garlands.

Tower Hill Botanic Garden

11 French Dr., Boylston, MA 01505
(508) 869-6111
towerhillbg.org

AREA: 129 acres
HOURS: Tues.–Sun. 10–5
ADMISSION: $15
AMENITIES:
EVENTS: Annual plant sale, classes, many events throughout the year

Founded in 1842, the Worcester County Horticultural Society is the third-oldest active horticultural society in the United States. In 1986 it purchased Tower Hill Farm in Boylston, to develop as a botanic garden. With majestic views of Wachusett Mountain and Reservoir, 130 acres of fields and woodlands, and a historic farmstead, the property was ideal. Today, Tower Hill is a horticultural showplace that exhibits exquisite plants and gorgeous planting combinations in 17 distinct gardens, and offers educational and recreational programs for the public.

Sited next to the farmhouse, the intimate Cottage Garden was the first to be developed at Tower Hill. It incorporates peonies, bearded iris, daylilies, and a double-flowered narcissus preserved from the original farmhouse, as well as newer ornamental

trees, shrubs, and flowers. A mature Japanese umbrella pine towers next to the house.

The Lawn Garden is planted with more than 350 species and hybrids of exquisite woody plants, along with thousands of spring bulbs, groundcovers, daylilies, peonies, and dahlias. This garden is stunning in fall, with the drama of brightly colored leaves, and in winter, when the beauty of bark, berries, and form stand out.

The Secret Garden is hidden from view on the lowest terrace of the Lawn Garden beyond the pergola. The oval garden is encircled with flower borders of fragrant perennials and annuals and anchored by a pool with a ram's head fountain.

Walking through the Visitor's Center, you reach the Systematic Garden, which illustrates plant relationships and 26 distinct plant families. Although primarily educational, the garden is beautifully designed in a playful Italianate style, with a fountain of volcanic rock and a central pergola painted in green and purple.

The newest garden at Tower Hill is The Court, a universally accessible space featuring beautiful plantings and fountains, artistic screens, and innovative moveable planters for mobility-challenged gardeners.

Enclosed on three sides by the building, the Winter Garden is protected from wind and extreme temperatures. The focal point is Domitian's Pool, with oversize Eastern Box Turtle fountains that delight visitors. The adjacent Orangerie and Limonaia are packed with citrus trees, winter-blooming tropical, and fragrant tender plants, and are a delight to visit on cold winter days. With robust programming and a diversity of garden spaces, Tower Hill is a destination year-round.

Garden Vision

10 Templeton Rd., Phillipston, MA 01331
(978) 249-3863
epimediums.com

HOURS: Select May weekends: see website
AMENITIES:

Garden Vision is a small mail-order nursery that has specialized in epimediums since 1997. Like other plant species, epimediums have developed collector status, and Garden Vision is fondly referred to as the "Epi-Center of the Universe."

The plants here represent the work of epimedium hybridizer and plant hunter Darrell Probst. He has spent the past two decades amassing the world's largest epimedium collection through expeditions to China, Japan, and Korea, networking with many other collectors, nurserymen, and experts worldwide, and developing his own hybrids. The nursery is now run by Karen Perkins, who continues to offer Probst's new introductions.

Garden Vision offers more than 200 epimedium hybrids for sale. The home nursery is open to the public for only a select few weekends in May during bloom season. They also sell epimediums at various plant sales throughout the Northeast.

Bridge of Flowers

22 Water St., Shelburne Falls, MA 01370
bridgeofflowersmass.org

AREA: 400 foot long bridge

HOURS: April–Oct: daily dawn–dusk

ADMISSION: Free

EVENTS: Annual plant sale in May, Bridge of Flowers 10k race in August

This flower-laden bridge has been blooming in Shelburne Falls for almost 90 years. Built in 1908 by the Shelburne Falls & Colrain Street Railway, the 400-foot concrete bridge spans the Deerfield River, connecting the towns of Shelburne and Buckland. It was originally built to deliver heavy freight from the Shelburne Falls rail yard to the mills across the river. The railway company, however, fell victim to the rise of the automobile, and went bankrupt in 1927.

For two years following the demise of the railway, the bridge lay overgrown with weeds. Residents were unsure what to do with it. It could not be torn down because it carried an essential water main between the two towns. Local resident Antoinette Burnham was determined to transform the eyesore into a "bridge of beauty." The Shelburne Falls Fire District purchased the bridge in 1929, and, with support from the community, the Women's Club assumed responsibility for its beautification. Volunteers helped install 80 truckloads of loam and fertilizer onto the bridge, and plants were donated from local gardens.

Today the Shelburne Falls Woman's Club continues to maintain the Bridge of Flowers. The plantings present a perfect example of a mixed border. The woody backbone consists of blooming ornamental trees—including magnolias, dogwoods, crabapples, redbuds, and cherries—as well as less common varieties such as the Golden Chain Tree, Seven Son's Flower, and Japanese Snowbell. Azaleas, pieris, weigelas, kolwitzia, and hydrangeas provide a flowering shrubby layer. A couple of wisterias and clematis form arbors over the bridge. Hundreds of sun-loving perennials—including gorgeous peonies, Siberian iris and poppies—along with colorful annuals and bulbs keep the Bridge in bloom from spring through fall. Every year, thousands of visitors from all over the world come to admire the Bridge and take away happy memories of a cunning landmark.

The Mount

2 Plunkett St., Lenox, MA 01240
(413) 551-5111
edithwharton.org

AREA: 113 acres

HOURS: May 13–Oct. 31: daily 10–5

ADMISSION: $18

AMENITIES:

EVENTS: Various tours and exhibits

Edith Wharton, author of *The Age of Innocence, Ethan Frome,* and *The House of Mirth*, became one of America's greatest writers at a time when women were discouraged from achieving anything beyond a proper marriage. She wrote more than 40 books in 40 years, and was the first woman awarded the Pulitzer Prize for Fiction. Inspired by her travels in Europe, Wharton also wrote authoritative works on architecture, gardens, interior design, and travel, and became an arbiter of taste in American society during the Gilded Age.

In 1901, eager to escape her home in Newport, Wharton bought 113-acres in Lenox and worked with Ogden Codman, Jr., and Francis L.V. Hoppin on the design of The Mount, a classically inspired house that would meet her needs as designer, gardener, hostess, and writer. The Mount is an example of the Country Place Era, a period from about 1890 to 1930. At this time, both architects and landscape designers were much in demand and re-

ceived large commissions from wealthy Americans who wanted to emulate English estates—to lend a sense of age and tradition to what in many cases was new money.

In 1904, Wharton published *Italian Villas and Their Gardens*, in which she advocated that gardens should be divided into rooms, a concept she used in designing The Mount's landscape. The mansion's main living spaces open onto a terrace offering a grand vista to Laurel Lake and the hills beyond. A Palladian stair descends from the terrace and leads to an allée of pleached lindens known as the Lime Walk, flanked by two formal gardens.

The sunken Italian Garden, with its porticos and alcoves in the stone walls, creates a cool respite from summer sun. The centerpiece of this garden is a rustic rock-pile fountain surrounded by ferns. Climbing hydrangea and white astilbe create a serene palette of greens and whites.

The French Flower Garden is planted with colorful shrubs and flowers—peonies, alliums, Siberian iris, petunias, phlox, snapdragons, stock, lilies, hydrangea, dianthus, delphinium, dahlias, and hollyhocks. The garden beds surround a rectangular pool with a dolphin fountain. The ornate latticework niche was designed by Codman, and was reconstructed from a photo.

Next to the formal terrace are grass steps descending into the gardens—a landscape feature rarely seen in America and part of Wharton's original design. They are surrounded with flowering shrubs and the many varieties of native ferns that Wharton personally collected around the Berkshires. Her niece, landscape gardener Beatrix Farrand, designed the estate's kitchen garden and the winding entrance drive planted with sugar maples and ostrich ferns. The Mount's landscape is beautiful at all times of the year, reflecting

Wharton's belief that the garden should possess "a charm independent of the seasons."

The original gardens at The Mount vanished through neglect over the decades, but have been meticulously restored at a cost of more than $3 million. Along with restoration of the hardscape, 5,000 trees, shrubs, and perennials were replanted according to Wharton's design. Restored to its former glory, The Mount welcomes more than 40,000 visitors every year.

Chesterwood

4 Williamsville Rd., Stockbridge, MA 02162
(413) 298-3579
chesterwood.org

AREA: 15 acres

HOURS: Memorial Day–Columbus Day: daily 10–5

ADMISSION: $18

AMENITIES:

EVENTS: Annual contemporary sculpture exhibit

Chesterwood was the home of Daniel Chester French, one of the most successful sculptors of the twentieth century, best known for his statue of Abraham Lincoln at the Lincoln Memorial in Washington, D.C. French purchased the 150-acre property in the Berkshires in 1896 for a summer estate and studio. He had already achieved national prominence for his bronze *Minute Man* statue, which resides at the Old North Bridge in Concord, Massachusetts. At Chesterwood he collaborated with his friend Henry Bacon on the construction of a residence and what would become his primary studio space for the rest of his career. The Colonial Revival house with its long veranda was sited to take advantage of the views of Monument Mountain and Mount Everett.

The main garden area is adjacent to the studio. French would often end a day of sculpting with a couple of hours tending the garden. A semicircular graveled courtyard is furnished with decorative planters and a pair of curved marble benches called exedras. Bacon designed the central marble-cement fountain for which French created putti relief. From the courtyard, marble steps lead to an elevated lawn with a central walk of peonies and *Hydrangea paniculata* standards. The main axis of the garden features a long perennial border planted with pastel-colored flowers. At its end, a pair of white-glazed terracotta columns mark the beginning of a woodland walk. The garden is enclosed by a lilac hedge and hemlocks, and accessorized with a pergola, marble benches, statuary, and a small square pool of water hyacinths and water lilies.

Chesterwood opened to the public in 1955, and in 1962 French's nephew, landscape architect Prentiss French, designed a new circulation pattern to better accommodate visitors. Today, Chesterwood is owned by the National Trust for Historic Preservation, which uses the grounds as exhibition space for contemporary sculpture as well as works by French. The studio, barn, and other gallery spaces include sculptural studies for a number of his works, including *The Minute Man*, *The Continents*, and *Abraham Lincoln*.

Naumkeag

5 Prospect Hill Rd., Stockbridge, MA 01262
(413) 298-8138
thetrustees.org/places-to-visit/berkshires/naumkeag.html

AREA: 48 acres

HOURS: April 2–Memorial Day: Sat.–Sun. 10–5; Memorial Day–Oct. 10: daily 10–5

ADMISSION: $15

AMENITIES:

EVENTS: Guided house tours

With its gracious house, striking gardens, and mountain views, Naumkeag is the quintessential Gilded Age country estate. Joseph Choate, a prominent New York City lawyer and ambassador to the United Kingdom, purchased the hillside property and hired his architect friend Charles McKim to design and build a 44-room, Shingle Style "cottage," for the family's summer retreat. The original gardens were Victorian in style with formal linear pathways and topiaries.

The eclectic modernist gardens that you see at Naumkeag today are the result of a 30-year collaboration between Choates' daughter, Mabel, and Boston designer Fletcher Steele. Mabel Choate, then 55 and a seasoned world traveler, met the forward-thinking landscape architect at a Lenox Garden Club gathering in the summer of 1926. The two formed an intense working relationship, which resulted in a series of inventive gardens filled with movement, color, and fantasy.

Steele favored modern features such as sweeping, undulating lines and strong color, but he believed a garden, even a new one, should have an antique patina. The intimate Afternoon Garden was the first he created for Naumkeag. It was designed to be seen from above, and features an intricate parterre with beds of pink gravel, scallop-shaped fountains, a grape arbor, and great pots of fuchsias. Brightly painted Venetian gondola posts connected by rope swags enclose this playful garden.

When Choate asked Steele for a new staircase down to her cutting garden, he created the dramatic Blue Steps, which are Naumkeag's most famous feature. The steps descend through groves of birches, their Art Deco-style curving white balustrades set off by dark green yews. Tiered fountain pools are highlighted by blue arcs. For years these arcs had been painted a robin's egg blue. During the recent restoration, it was discovered that they were supposed to be a deep navy.

The Rose Garden was designed to be viewed from Choates' bedroom. It consists of 16 scallop-shaped beds arranged in a zigzag pattern, each containing a different Floribunda rose. The rose beds are joined with swirling ribbons of pink gravel.

After a trip to China in 1935, Choate added Asian elements to the garden. First the Tree Peony Terrace was installed on the slope behind the

house, with 60 varieties planted on three fieldstone terraces. The walled Chinese Garden took 20 years to complete, and features a blue-tiled temple, ginkos underplanted with petasites, stone lions, and numerous Asian plants. The circular moon gate added in 1955 was Steele's last contribution to the estate.

In 1958 Naumkeag was bequeathed in its entirety to The Trustees of Reservations. Spurred by a sizeable gift, a $3 million garden restoration was completed in 2016. Thanks to Steele's meticulous records, notes and plant lists, the gardens were replanted according to his original design. The fountains and hardscapes were restored, overgrown trees and shrubs removed, and 250 new trees planted. Today, the garden is as Choate and Steele designed it—an unconventional and whimsical collaboration between two kindred spirits.

Berkshire Botanical Garden

5 West Stockbridge Rd., Stockbridge, MA 02162
(413) 298-3926
berkshirebotanical.org

AREA: 15 acres

HOURS: May 1–Columbus Day: daily 9–5

ADMISSION: $15

AMENITIES:

EVENTS: Plant sale, Flower Show, Harvest Fair, lectures, exhibits, art classes & more

For more than 80 years, the Berkshire Botanical Garden (BBG) has grown and prospered due to the generosity of local supporters who believe a botanical garden is not only a place of serenity and beauty, but an essential component of a healthy community.

The Garden was established in 1934 by the Lenox Garden Club on a parcel of land with a 1790 farmhouse donated by Bernhard and Irene Hoffman. Other public gardens donated plants, including a noteworthy collection of prized daylilies from the New York Botanical Garden. During World War II, the BBG installed a Victory Garden to teach families how to augment their government rations by growing vegetables and fruits. Classes were also offered in canning, freezing, and winter storage, and at the end of the war, the Garden received a National Victory Garden Institute Award in recognition of its "contribution to the national war effort."

Today's BBG has educational programs for home gardeners, landscape professionals, and children, along with 26 beautiful themed display gardens with plants that are indigenous to or thrive in the Berkshires. The Entry Garden is particularly stunning in late summer, with towering perennials, grasses, castor bean plants, purple-leaved cannas, and black elephant ears. The Children's Flower and Vegetable Garden is framed with rustic pergolas and planted with bright flowers and colorful produce. The Martha Stewart Garden features an adorable garden shed topped with a succulent-covered roof and surrounded by an exuberant cottage garden. The formal Rose Garden exhibits hardy roses, fragrant David Austin introductions, and old-fashioned varieties.

There are several perennial gardens on the property, some focusing on sun-lovers, others on shady plants. A shady Hosta Garden displays many hybrids interplanted with ferns and other woodland plants. An American Daylily Society Display Garden features more than 200 cultivars, planted chronologically by date of introduction. The Herb Garden, built in 1937 on a terraced rocky slope, is planted with 100 varieties of hardy and tender herbs displayed according to use, plant family, and ornamental value. The recently renovated Pond Garden with its trickling waterfall showcases plants that thrive with wet feet. The Berkshire Botanical Garden is a font of inspiration from spring through fall.

Berkshire Botanical Garden

Campo de' Fiori

1815 N. Main Street, Sheffield, MA 01257
(413) 528-1857
campodefiori.com

HOURS: Daily 10–5
AMENITIES:

Campo de' Fiori is known for its Italian-inspired, moss-covered, hand-made terra-cotta pots. The creators of this line, Robin Norris and his wife, Barbara Bockbrader, are dedicated to simple, handcrafted garden accessories that are both functional and beautiful. Their shop carries an irresistible collection of hand-forged iron trellises, stakes, and brackets, as well as rustic garden ornaments, hand-carved stone planters and animals, garden lanterns and light fixtures, unusual outdoor furniture, and botanically-inspired gifts and decorative items.

Norris designs the pots, planters, and accessories, and oversees their production in Mexico. These objects—whether clay pots, hand-forged steel or blown glass, are all crafted using traditional methods. Bockbrader, a horticulturalist by training, combines unusual plants with the vessels her husband creates. You will see large pots of towering brugmansias, hydrangeas, and cannas adorning the porch. Tiny ferns sprout from mossy terracotta pots, and succulents bask in a hand-carved stone bowls. Bockbrader also maintains the lush gardens that engulf the shop and are adorned with unique statuary and Campo de' Fiori originals crafted from wood, concrete, iron, bronze, and terracotta.

Ashintully

Sodem Rd., Tyringham, MA 01264
(413) 298-3239
thetrustees.org/places-to-visit/berkshires/ashintully-gardens.html

AREA: 120 acres

HOURS: June–mid Oct.: Wed. & Sat. 1–5

ADMISSION: Free

EVENTS: Garden tours for 15 or more, fees apply

In 1903, Egyptologist Robb de Peyster Tytus and his wife Grace discovered the Tyringham Valley on their honeymoon. They purchased 1,000 acres, named it Ashintully (Gaelic meaning "on the brow of the hill"), and built a 35-room Georgian-style

mansion. Locals came to call it the Marble Palace because of the way the pure white stucco reflected the sunlight. In 1952, the house burned down in a forest fire triggered by drought, but four Doric columns testify to a bygone era. The present-day ruins command a striking view of the distant Berkshire Hills.

The Tytus's son, contemporary composer John McLennan, acquired the property in 1937 and moved to the farmhouse at the bottom of the hill. Ashintully Gardens is his 30-year creation—a serene retreat in the Berkshires surrounded by forested hills and traversed by a rushing stream. When McLennan began gardening on the property, it was completely overgrown with brush and weed trees. He slowly cleared the land, creating one garden area at a time, with no master plan. A self-educated gardener with a keen eye for spatial relationships, elegant form, and proportion, McLennan was particularly interested in contrasts—light and shade, large open spaces and small, enclosed areas, and the juxtaposition of the natural and the formal. He let the natural aspects of the site—the sloping landforms, stately trees and existing water features—guide his design choices. The gardens blend these natural features with formal elements such as straight walkways, shaped arborvitae, and dramatic fountains. Overall, the gardens are an exercise in restraint. The plant palette is restricted to yews, arborvitae, and ivy. The color palette is green and white with pots of geraniums that serve as colorful accents. Urns, columns, and statuary are strategically placed to ornament the garden.

The remains of the Tytus's mansion are accessible via a steep climb on a trail through the woods. Good walking shoes are a must, as the trail is fraught with roots and rocks and may be slippery when wet.

Rhode Island

SUGGESTED DAILY ITINERARIES

Morning

Shakespeare Head Garden, Providence (1)

Roger Williams Park Botanical Center, Providence (2)

Lunch–Quito's Restaurant, Bristol

Blithewold, Bristol (3)

Morning

Green Animals, Portsmouth (4)

Lunch–Carolyn's Sakonnet Vineyard, Little Compton

Carolyn's Sakonnet Vineyard, Little Compton (6)

Peckham's Nursery, Little Compton (5)

Morning

The Breakers, Newport (8)

Lunch–Michael's, Newport

The Elms, Newport (9)

Rosecliff, Newport (7)

Morning

Kinney Azalea Gardens, South Kingston (10)

The Farmer's Daughter, South Kingston (11)

Rhode Island

Roger Williams Park Botanical Center

1000 Elmwood Ave., Providence, RI 02905
(401) 785-9450
providenceri.com/botanical-center

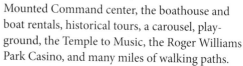

AREA: 12,000 sq. ft. of greenhouses

HOURS: Tues. –Sun. 11–4

ADMISSION: $5

AMENITIES:

EVENTS: Concerts, annual plant sale, fairy garden days, photo contest

Roger Williams Park was created in 1870 after Betsey Williams bequeathed 102 acres of farmland and woodland to the city of Providence to be used for public purpose. A portion of the gift included land that was originally purchased from the Narragansetts by her great, great, great, grandfather, Rhode Island's founder Roger Williams.

Horace Cleveland, a leader in the Urban Parks Movement, created the design for the park. It was intended to serve as an escape for residents of highly industrialized Providence in the late 19th century. Today, the Roger Williams Park contains a zoo, a museum of natural history, a planetarium, the Botanical Center, Japanese Gardens, Victorian Rose Gardens, the Providence Police Department's Mounted Command center, the boathouse and boat rentals, historical tours, a carousel, playground, the Temple to Music, the Roger Williams Park Casino, and many miles of walking paths.

The Botanical Center opened in 2007, and at 12,000 square feet is the largest public indoor display garden in New England. It includes two main greenhouses: The Conservatory and the Mediterranean Room. The Conservatory has the feeling of a large courtyard surrounded by elegant tall palms. Unlike most greenhouses, this one is airy and open, with a central area for ceremonies or social events. A fountain bubbles and colorful tropical plants bloom beneath stately trees. Immense birds of paradise hide among the palms, like storks in the jungle. The Mediterranean Room is built around a long stucco wall with a circular gate. A densely planted pond with giant koi dominates the room. The Orchid Society displays delicate orchids growing in a moss-draped tree in one corner, and the Carnivorous Plant Society exhibits pitcher plants and delicate wild flowers in a raised bog garden. A small waterfall and a Mediterranean fountain provide soothing background music. All in all, there are over 150 different species and cultivars of plants including 17 types of palms. Upcoming projects include a Flavor Lab designed for chefs and farmers to compare the taste of vegetable varieties, and a Journey Through America exhibit featuring plants native to South, Central, and North America.

The Botanical Center's outdoor display gardens are equally attractive. The Winter Garden has gorgeous specimens of umbrella pines, a Lacebark Pine, Metasequoia, and other unusual conifers; Sargent cherries and trees with distinctive bark such river birches; hellebores, evergreen ferns, and bamboo. Other displays include a beautiful Perennial Garden, with large plantings of bee balm, balloon flower, phlox, daylilies, coneflowers, and

blackeye susans. A Pine and Hosta Dell, Wooded Hillside Garden, Overlook Terrace, and Rain Garden offer interesting plantings to view. Downhill from the greenhouses, gorgeous roses and clematis cover the arches of the Rose Maze.

Blithewold

101 Ferry Rd., Bristol, RI 02809
(401) 253-2707
blithewold.org

AREA: 33 acres
HOURS: Gardens: daily dawn-dusk; mansion: April–
Columbus Day: Tues.–Sun. 10–4
ADMISSION: $15; Grounds free Jan.–March
AMENITIES:
EVENTS: Christmas at Blithewold, workshops, lectures,
daffodil display, teas

Overlooking Narragansett Bay, Blithewold is an excellent example of the "Country Place Era." The 33-acre summer estate features an elegant 45-room mansion set among gardens that range in character from mysterious to exotic and from poetic to practical.

In 1895 Augustus Van Wickle and his wife, Bessie, purchased 70 acres on the Bristol waterfront, and named it Blithewold (Old English for "happy woodland"). There they eschewed Newport's glitz and grandeur and instead built a large, Queen Anne style summer home. They hired landscape architect John DeWolf to design a horticultural sanctuary. With Bessie's involvement, DeWolf designed 33 acres of display gardens, a great lawn, an arboretum of specimen trees, a rose garden, a rock garden, a water garden, and a bosquet. Vegetable and cutting gardens supplied the house.

Just three years after purchasing the property, Augustus was killed in a skeet-shooting accident. Bessie remarried in 1901, but five years later fire completely destroyed the house. The following year she built a second, grander mansion on the site in an English Country Manor style—that is the mansion you can visit today. Work continued on the grounds with the addition of rare trees, including a now-90-foot-tall giant sequoia, stone walls, and a formal perennial garden.

Bessie's daughter, Marjorie, was married in the enclosed garden, and spent the rest of her life at Blithewold. An avid gardener like her mother, she continued implementing the master plan for the

Augusts and Bessie

property, developing the arboretum and cultivating rare plants. When Marjorie died in 1976, she left the estate to the Heritage Trust of Rhode Island. Without financial resources to maintain the property, the trust prepared to sell it to a private developer, however a small group of local citizens banded together and raised $650,000 to save the estate. They formed Save Blithewold, a nonprofit organization that now maintains the house and garden. Thanks to their efforts and the estate's archives, you can enjoy Blithewold's gardens as they were designed 100 years ago.

Blithewold is beautiful in all seasons. In early spring more than 50,000 daffodils and native woodland wildflowers delight visitors in the bosquet. Bessie's favorite, the Rock Garden, features miniature irises, primroses, and other alpine favorites. The Rose Garden is stunning in early summer with climbing and shrub roses, the centenarian Chestnut Rose from Mt. Vernon, and an Asian-inspired moon gate. The Water Garden—with its arched stone bridge, water lilies, flag iris, and Japanese maples—is glorious in midsummer. The Bamboo Grove is a favorite with children and adults alike. A Nut Grove features Manchurian walnuts, bitternut, butternut, hickory, and Chinese chestnuts. No matter when you visit, Blithewold is romantic, fresh, and inspiring.

Green Animals Topiary Garden

380 Corys Ln., Portsmouth, RI 02871
(401) 683-1267
newportmansions.org/explore/green-animals-topiary-garden

AREA: 7 acres

HOURS: Open daily, see website

ADMISSION: $17.50

AMENITIES:

EVENTS: House tours

With more than 80 whimsical topiaries sculpted from California privet, yew, and English boxwood, Green Animals is the oldest and northernmost topiary garden in the United States. The small country estate overlooking Narragansett Bay was purchased in 1872 by Thomas E. Brayton, treasurer of the Union Cotton Manufacturing Company in Fall River, Massachusetts. It included a white clapboard summer residence, farm outbuildings, a pasture, and a vegetable garden.

Brayton's daughter Alice gave the estate its name because of the profusion of "green animals" created by property superintendent Joseph Carreiro, who designed and maintained the ornamental and edible gardens from 1905 to 1945. He experimented with California privet propagated in the estate greenhouse, and developed a system for training privet into oversize animal shapes without the support of frames. Many of the animals took

almost 20 years to grow into their final size. Since Green Animals was a summer residence, it was not a concern that privet is deciduous and sheds its leaves in the fall. Carriero's son-in-law, George Mendonca, took over as superintendent until 1985 and expanded the gardens to include more than 80 topiaries, sculpted from privet, yew, and boxwood.

Alice Brayton inherited the estate and made it her permanent residence. An avid historian and gardener, she bequeathed Green Animals to The Preservation Society of Newport County upon her death. Today, Green Animals remains as a rare example of an estate with formal topiaries, beautiful flower, vegetable, and herb gardens, orchards, and a Victorian house.

The landscape is a series of garden rooms bordered by mature conifers and magnolias. The fanciful topiaries are the stars. Favorites include teddy bears, a camel, a giraffe, an ostrich, an elephant, a unicorn, a reindeer, a dog, and a horse with his rider. They are set within flowerbeds planted with colorful perennials and annuals. Near the house and main entrance, the topiary retains a more formal style of figurative and geometric shapes. A walkway of arched topiary leads around the house to the front porch, where you can relax on a rocking chair and enjoy a view of the bay. The topiaries are all pruned by hand using garden shears and require weekly trimming to look their best. Some conservation metal supports have been discreetly positioned inside the forms to provide stability in wind and snow.

The rest of the garden is equally magical with grape arbors, fruit beds, orchards, and elaborate cutting gardens. The vegetable garden sports whimsical scarecrows that delight children. The Brayton house museum contains a display of vintage toys, including a large collection of toy soldiers and vintage dollhouses. Adults will appreciate the original Victorian family furnishings and

decoration. Ribbons for prize-winning dahlias and vegetables, dating from about 1915, line the walls of the charming gift shop.

Peckham's Greenhouse

200 W. Main Rd., Little Compton, RI 02837
(401) 635-4775
peckhamsgreenhouse.com

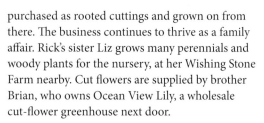

HOURS: May 1–June 30: daily 9–5; July 1–Dec. 23:
Tues–Sun. 9–5

AMENITIES: 👪 🚻

EVENTS: Various sales and special events

Peckham's Greenhouse is a historic fixture in rural Little Compton, with pastoral views of fields, grazing cattle and the Sakonnet River. The Peckham family started a dairy and vegetable farm on the land in 1865. The farm is now run by fifth-generation plantsman Rick Peckham, and has evolved into a vibrant nursery offering flowering annuals, vegetable starts, perennials, and hardy shrubs. The garden center covers five acres, more than 20,000 square feet of which are heated greenhouses—some, the original structures.

Peckham's grows just about everything from scratch. In most years, they seed and grow over 300 varieties of annuals. Other annuals are purchased as rooted cuttings and grown on from there. The business continues to thrive as a family affair. Rick's sister Liz grows many perennials and woody plants for the nursery, at her Wishing Stone Farm nearby. Cut flowers are supplied by brother Brian, who owns Ocean View Lily, a wholesale cut-flower greenhouse next door.

Rick and his employees are generous with their time and expertise. They want customers to succeed and enjoy gardening. They will answer questions about the plants they sell and give advice about issues that you may be experiencing in your garden. Do you have a sickly houseplant? Bring it to Peckham's for pruning and repotting in their premium potting mix. Are your pruners dull? Peckham's will sharpen them for you. Looking for alpines? Rick will find them for you. When you visit Peckham's, you are treated like family.

Carolyn's Sakonnet Vineyard

162 W Main Rd., Little Compton, RI 02837
(401) 635-8486
sakonnetwine.com

AREA: Vineyard is 30 acres.
HOURS: Daily 11–6; Fri. & Sat. 11–8
AMENITIES: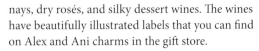
EVENTS: Free tour, wine tastings, summer concert series, Sunday afternoon jazz series

For a different garden touring experience, visit Carolyn's Sakonnet Vineyard, located on 150 acres in a charming corner of Little Compton. Thirty acres of the winery are currently under cultivation and are planted with chardonnay, gewürztraminer, pinot noir, cabernet franc, and vidal blanc grapes. The vineyard—founded in 1975 and purchased by Alex and Ani LLC in 2012—is nestled between Watson Reservoir and the Sakonnet River. The soil conditions and maritime location closely resemble those of northern France, and the cool air combines with a humid subtropical climate, resulting in a longer ripening season and a later harvest. Sakonnet's grapes are slow to develop and mature into fruits with low sugar levels and high acidity. These grapes are handpicked and aged in oak barrels, resulting in full-bodied reds, crisp chardonnays, dry rosés, and silky dessert wines. The wines have beautifully illustrated labels that you can find on Alex and Ani charms in the gift store.

In addition to touring the vineyard, you can enjoy perennial gardens around the winery building and a long perennial border with stunning water views in the back of the property. The café serves delicious meals made from fresh, local ingredients served at picnic tables under an ancient shade tree. You can follow this with a tasting of seven wines made on the property. In the summer, end the day with an outdoor concert in the field.

Rosecliff Mansion

548 Bellevue Ave., Newport, RI 02840
(401) 847-1000
newportmansions.org/explore/rosecliff

AREA: 21 acres
HOURS: Open daily, see website
ADMISSION: $17.50
AMENITIES:
EVENTS: Various tours available; Newport Flower Show

"Inspired by a French king's garden retreat, built by a legendary Newport hostess, and designed by one of the Gilded Age's most flamboyant architects, a sense of theater and fantasy pervades the atmosphere and every detail of Rosecliff."

–John Tschirch, architectural historian

Rosecliff is an exquisite mansion clad in white glazed terracotta tiles that are adorned with cascades of flowers and musical instruments. Architect Stanford White designed the mansion for Nevada silver heiress Tessie Oelrichs, who bought the property in 1891. White modeled it after the Grand Trianon, the royal garden retreat at Versailles. After the house was completed in 1902, at a staggering cost of $2.5 million, Oelrichs hosted lavish themed parties, complete with celebrity entertainers.

In 1971 Rosecliff, its furnishings, and an endowment were donated to the Preservation Society of Newport by its last private owners, Mr. and Mrs. J. Edgar Monroe, of New Orleans. Several movies—including The Great Gatsby, True Lies, Amistad, and 27 Dresses—have been made at the mansion.

Appropriately, a small rose garden bordered by a pergola is the main garden feature at Rosecliff. The noted horticulturalist George Bancroft owned the original wooden cottage called Rosecliff on the property, which Oelrichs replaced with the current mansion. Bancroft's rose cuttings were used to develop the American Beauty rose, the signature flower of the Gilded Age. The back of the mansion features terraces overlooking a pool with fountain and a stunning ocean view.

For the past twenty years, Rosecliff has hosted the Newport Flower Show in late June. With beautiful gardens recreated on the front lawn and floral arrangements throughout the house, this is a wonderful opportunity to enjoy botanical splendor at Rosecliff.

The Breakers

44 Ochre Point Ave., Newport, RI 02840
(401) 847-1000
newportmansions.org/explore/the-breakers

AREA: 21 acres

HOURS: Open daily, see website

ADMISSION: $17.50

AMENITIES:

EVENTS: Various tours available

The Breakers is the grandest of Newport's summer "cottages," a prime example of the Gilded Age, and the most visited attraction in Rhode Island. It was the summer home of Cornelius Vanderbilt II, grandson of Commodore Cornelius Vanderbilt, the steamship and railroad baron who established the family fortune. Cornelius II purchased a wooden house called The Breakers in Newport during in 1885. When the original house burned down in 1892, he commissioned esteemed architect Richard Morris Hunt to design a grand and fireproof villa. The resulting 70-room palazzo was inspired by Renaissance palaces of Genoa and Turin. The interiors were designed by Odgen Codman, Jr., and Jules Allard and Sons, and feature marble from Italy and Africa, rare woods, intricate mosaics, and architectural elements from European chateaux.

The gardens were designed by Ernest W. Bowditch, a protégé of Frederick Law Olmstead. Bowditch personally selected many of the rare trees for the property, particularly the beeches. Newport was the stage for horticultural experimentation and garden design during the 19th century, and technological advances in cast iron and glass greenhouses, and global expeditions enabled the cultivation and dissemination of exotic trees and plants. Newport's estate gardeners had to import almost all of their trees since the indigenous tree population had disappeared with the clearing of land for sheep farming in the 18th century.

The Breakers' pea-gravel driveway is lined with mature pin oaks and red maples. Plantings of arborvitae, yew, Chinese juniper, and dwarf hemlock create an attractive perimeter around the formally landscaped terrace. Clipped hedges of Japanese yew and Pfitzer juniper line the footpaths that wind through the grounds. The property is enclosed with a beautiful wrought iron fence and borders of flowering shrubs and trees such as rhododendron, mountain laurels, and dogwoods that screen the grounds from street traffic and provide privacy within.

You can see Bowditch's original pattern for the south parterre garden, which has been recreated from old photographs in pink and white begonias and blue ageratum. The north garden features a fountain and parterre beds of salvia, marigolds, and ageratum. Stone balustrades and formal urns frame the dramatic ocean views in the back of the mansion.

Gladys Vanderbilt, the youngest daughter of the family, inherited the house and became an ardent supporter of The Preservation Society of Newport County. She opened The Breakers to the public in 1948 to raise funds for the Society, and in 1972 the Preservation Society purchased the house and the majority of its contents from her heirs.

The Elms

367 Bellevue Ave., Newport, RI 02840
(401) 847-1000
newportmansions.org/explore/the-elms

AREA: 11 acres

HOURS: Open daily, see website

ADMISSION: $17.50

AMENITIES:

EVENTS: Various tours available

The Elms is one of the grandest mansions in Newport, and was built by Mr. and Mrs. Edward Julius Berwind of Philadelphia and New York. Like many other Newport residents, the Berwinds were "new money," having made their fortune in the coal industry. They hired Philadelphia architect Horace Trumbauer to design a summer estate modeled after the mid-18th -century French chateau d'Asnieres. Construction of The Elms was completed in 1901 at reported cost of $1.4 million.

The gardens of The Elms were developed from 1902 to 1914 under the direction of Trumbauer, who produced the drawings and plans for the grand allée, marble pavilions, and sunken garden.

The gardens were originally conceived as a place for staging grand entertainments and as an outdoor sculpture gallery, with several large pieces by European sculptors.

The Elms is a prime example of the Classical Revival Style in architecture and landscape design. During the late 1880s, both patrons and architects were attracted to French classicism as a new approach for estates with formal, aristocratic pretensions. Newport had become the most fashionable summer resort, and therefore the logical site for the American version of the maison de plaisance, or pleasure pavilion, a French concept that idealized a perfect unification of house and garden. At The Elms, the terraces ease the transition from the ballroom to the open air. They also provide a platform from which viewers could observe the garden.

From 1902 to 1907, the gardens were a picturesque

park with specimen trees and a small lily pond. After 1907, the garden underwent changes due to newer theories in American landscape architecture. In the early 20th century, tastes in America became heavily influenced by Charles Adams Platt and Edith Wharton, both of whom published works exhorting Italian villas and their gardens. Stylish Americans adapted their country estates by adding gravel-lined forecourts, planted terracing, formal stairs and water features, herbaceous borders, and pergolas. Trumbauer reworked The Elms's garden to reflect this new revival of classical Italian design. The pond became the present sunken garden at the back of the estate. Viewed from the terraces and summerhouses, the intricate patterning of annuals, ivy, yews, and euonymous is delightful.

The American elms, after which the property was named, succumbed to Dutch elm disease in the early 1970s and were replaced by weeping beeches. The Elms' garden was restored in 2001.

Kinney Azalea Gardens

2391 Kingstown Rd. (Rte 108), South Kingstown, RI 02879
(401) 782-8847

AREA: 6 acres of gardens, 2 acres of walking trails
HOURS: Daily dawn–dusk
ADMISSION: Free, donation accepted
AMENITIES:
EVENTS: Guided tours with Dr. Gordon by appointment

The Kinney Azalea Gardens are a hidden gem—a private garden that grew out of the horticultural passions of Lorenzo Kinney, Jr, who moved there with his wife, Elizabeth, in 1927. The first azalea and rhododendron plants were planted shortly, with help from Lorenzo's father, the first professor of botany at the nearby University of Rhode Island. Lorenzo inherited a love of horticulture from his father, and a love of plein air oil painting from his mother, who was URI's first painting professor. Lorenzo was able to pursue both in the creation of his garden. Azaleas became his passion after visiting Elizabeth's native Virginia and seeing the extensive azalea plantings in southern estates. At that time, there were few azaleas available for northern gardens, so Lorenzo began collecting azaleas from the southern U.S. and from around the world, and hybridizing his own—a hobby that turned into a second career. His hybrids, known as the K-series, can be seen on the K Path in the garden. A beautiful peach hybrid is named in honor of Elizabeth.

With help from many high school and college students, Lorenzo planted five acres of gardens. One of those high school students, Susan Gordon, went on to earn a doctorate in plant sciences. She worked extensively with Lorenzo from 1976 until his death in 1994 at the age of 100. Lorenzo's daughter and son-in-law, Betty and Tony Faella, now own the property and welcome visitors to their garden year-round. Susan Gordon manages the gardens and continues to develop new hybrids. She has planted a sixth acre as Galle's Footsteps, a series of seven footprints, each devoted to a hybridizer who built on the work of the late Fred C. Galle, a friend of Lorenzo's. She has also created naturalized areas with native shrubs and perennials to preserve the biodiversity of the garden.

The azaleas are at their peak from mid-May to early June, when the garden is ablaze in pink, white, red and coral. There are more than 800 cultivars and 30 species of azaleas to view, about 500 cultivars of rhododendrons, and collections of mountain laurel, boxwood, pieris, leucothoe, itea, calycanthus, and oakleaf hydrangeas. A stand of mature umbrella pines was a wedding gift to Lorenzo from his parents, and the moongate, a 10-foot circular stone arch, was built by local stonemasons for Tony's 75th birthday.

You can also purchase azaleas, rhododendrons, leucothoe, mountain laurel, and other shrubs, both in pots and as full-grown specimens from the garden. The nursery's proceeds fund the operations of the Kinney Azalea Gardens. Cash and check only.

Painting of the house and garden by Lorenzo Kinney (above)

The Farmer's Daughter

716 Mooresfield Rd., South Kingstown, RI 02879
(401) 792-1340
thefarmersdaughterri.com

PERENNIALS

HOURS: Mid-March–Dec.: daily 9–6
AMENITIES:
EVENTS: Workshops

Sarah Partyka grew up on a family farm, and learned the joys of vegetable and perennial gardening from her Polish and English grandmothers. Inspired by her family heritage, she earned a horticulture degree from University of Rhode Island, and launched The Farmer's Daughter in 1998. The business grew from a small shop and single greenhouse to a flourishing garden center in South County.

Today The Farmer's Daughter offers a great selection of annuals, heirloom veggies, herbs, and woodies, as well as a diverse selection of perennials. Most are grown on-site at the farm, and range from historical favorites to new varieties. You will find a nice selection of alpines—diminutive gems that are perfect for troughs, rock gardens and sunny spots. You can also buy plants that are perfect for seaside conditions and tolerate sandy soils, wind, and sea spray. Many of these tough perennials, often with thick succulent leaves or fuzzy foliage and deep root systems, are ideal for roadside conditions as well. You will also find annual starts for a cutting garden—tall cleome, snapdragons, cosmos, and zinnias in a myriad of colors. Lovely display gardens are enjoyed by gardeners and wedding parties.

The nursery is committed to sustainable agricultural methods: natural composts, organic ingredients, manures, and cover crops. All plants and produce are grown and harvested using traditional sustainable farming. Beautiful organic produce is available for sale in the summer months. The well-curated gift shop and greenhouses are full of inspirational ideas for the gardener.

Shakespeare's Head Garden

21 Meeting St., Providence, RI 02903
(401) 831-7440
ppsri.org/organization/shakespeare-s-head-garden

HOURS: Daily dawn–dusk
ADMISSION: Free

Located behind the building known as "Shakespeare's Head" and the John Carter House, this Colonial revival-style garden is a green oasis just steps from downtown Providence. The square, three-story building was built in 1772 by John Carter, postmaster and the publisher of the city's first newspaper, The Providence Gazette. Carter had apprenticed to Benjamin Franklin, who, as newly-appointed Postmaster General, assigned Carter to the position of Postmaster of Providence in 1767. Carter operated his press, Post Office, and bookshop on the ground floor, and lived with his family on the upper floors. Outside the building, a sign bearing Shakespeare's likeness advertised the literary enterprises within. The image may be gone, but the name has remained. The building now houses the Providence Preservation Society.

The existing garden was designed by James Graham in the Colonial revival style after the original garden was destroyed in the 1938 hurricane. It was later modified by landscape architect Lalla Searle of the Rhode Island School of Design for easier maintenance and historical accuracy. The garden is enclosed by stone walls and terraces, with brick-lined pathways. Four quince trees form the corners of the sunken garden, and a Japanese maple stands proudly in the center. The beds are planted with baptisia, columbines, foxgloves, goatsbeard, and other perennials. A long peony border and a row of pear trees outline the first terrace. The garden is most colorful in early June when the peonies and roses are in bloom.

Connecticut

SUGGESTED DAILY ITINERARIES

Morning
Logee's, Danielson (2)
Lunch–Thai Palace, Danielson
Roseland Cottage, Woodstock (1)

Morning
Elizabeth Park, W. Hartford (4)
Lunch–Elizabeth Park Pond House, W. Hartford
O'Brien Nurserymen, Granby (3)
Dinosaur State Park, Rocky Hill (5)

Morning
Florence Griswold Museum, Old Lyme (6)
Lunch–Florence Griswold Museum Café
Harkness Memorial State Park, Waterford (7)

Morning
Broken Arrow Nursery, Hamden (8)
Twombly Nursery, Monroe (9)
Lunch–Good News Café, Woodbury
Glebe House, Woodbury (11)
The Elemental Garden, Woodbury (12)
Hollandia Nursery, Bethel (10)

Morning
Bellamy-Ferriday House, Bethlehem (16)
Lunch–The Village Restaurant, Litchfield
Hollister House Garden, Washington (13)
White Flower Farm, Morris (15)

Morning
Hillstead Museum, Farmington (18)
Lunch–Apricot's, Farmington
Crickett Hill Garden, Thomaston (17)

Connecticut

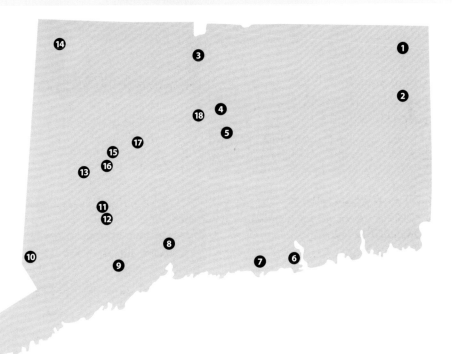

Roseland Cottage

556 Route 169, Woodstock, CT 06281
(860) 928-4074
historicnewengland.org/historic-properties/homes/roseland-cottage

AREA: 2 acres

HOURS: June 1–Oct. 15: Wed.–Sun. 11–4; closed July 4 and Columbus Day

ADMISSION: $10 adults

AMENITIES:

EVENTS: Tours on the hour, last tour at 4 pm; Fine Art and Craft Fair in October

Roseland Cottage offers an unparalleled glimpse into 19th century upper-class life in New England. New York City businessman Henry Bowen built the house in 1846 as a summer cottage for his family, in the quiet and scenic corner of Connecticut where he grew up.

Prominently situated across from the town common, the bright salmon pink cottage with its black trim epitomizes Gothic Revival architecture, with its steep gables, decorative bargeboards, and ornamented chimney pots. The interior is equally colorful and features elaborate wall coverings, heavily patterned carpets, and stained glass. Andrew Jackson Downing, the leading 19th century taste-maker, declared that the Gothic Revival's soaring, asymmetrical style suited a dynamic personality, which fit Bowen perfectly. A self-made business

leader, active abolitionist, and political manipulator, Bowen designed the cottage as a showplace to affirm his success. He used it to entertain friends and political connections, including four U.S. presidents.

The entire complex of house, furnishings, outbuildings, and landscape reflects Downing's principles. Bowen owned a copy of Downing's *A Treatise on the Theory and Practice of Landscape Gardening* and adhered to it as much as possible. Roseland's approach drive, though not very long, was lined with specimen trees that included a ginkgo, shagbark hickory, hawthorn, and a tulip tree, which continues to bloom beautifully to this day. The parterre garden was the landscape's crowning glory. Its 21 beds were thickly planted with colorful roses, perennials and annuals, and outlined with 600 yards of low boxwood. Historic New England continues to plant it in the Victorian bedding style, using more than 3,500 colorful annuals each year. The flowers reach their peak in mid-July. The garden's formal design, based on a fine carpet, is best appreciated when viewed from the upstairs windows of the house.

The estate also includes an icehouse, aviary, carriage barn, and the nation's oldest surviving indoor bowling alley.

Logee's Greenhouses

141 North St., Danielson, CT 06239
(860) 774-8038
logees.com

AREA: 6 greenhouses

HOURS: Daily 10–5

AMENITIES:

EVENTS: Winter tours for garden clubs, groups and schools

If you need a break from a long New England winter, visit Logee's Greenhouses, a family owned mail-order and retail business in northeastern Connecticut. You can enjoy a mini tropical vacation touring the six packed greenhouses on narrow paths overhung with luscious fragrant plants. The Fern House is the oldest, dating back to 1892, and features staghorns, tree ferns, and other unusual varieties. The Herb House contains herbs for culinary and medicinal uses, including unusual plants such as turmeric, cinnamon, allspice, and lemongrass. The walls of the Potting House are draped with many cultivars of passion flowers surrounding a display of spice plants and bonsai. The Big House is home to cacti, succulents, scented geraniums, camellias, and clivia. The centerpiece is a 150-year-old tree sporting ten varieties of oranges. The Long House bursts with Logee's hybrid begonias and a collection of blooming, rare, and fruiting plants. Are you looking for a fig tree? Logee's has 14 varieties, as well as pawpaws and hardy kiwis and bananas.

Logee's most famous resident occupies the Lemon Tree House along with orchids and other citrus plants. It is a giant 'Ponderosa' lemon tree that has grown there since 1900 and produces lemons the size of grapefruits. The company's founder, William D. Logee, purchased the tree in Philadelphia. It was known as the "American Wonder Lemon" due to the size of its fruit, which could get as large as five pounds. The tree was shipped via train, then picked up by horse and buggy, and planted directly into the ground in the original greenhouse. Thousands of propagations have been harvested and sold from this original tree.

The Logee family has run the business since its founding in 1892. William's eldest son, Ernest, hybridized begonias for Logee's and was one of the original founders of the American Begonia Society. Under his direction, Logee's at one time grew more than 400 varieties of begonias. The business is currently run by Byron Logee and Laurelynn Glass Martin, who continue to introduce a wide range of tropical, exotic, and fruiting plants to gardeners throughout the Unites States.

O'Brien Nurserymen

40 Wells Rd., Granby, CT 06035
(860) 653-0163
obrienhosta.com

HOURS: Check website for open times

AMENITIES: 👫

Ten years ago, O'Brien Nurserymen was already one of New England's premier hosta nurseries. Today, it is a plant collector's haven, with the most unusual and sought-after varieties of shade perennials, trees, and shrubs.

John O'Brien is an extremely friendly, knowledgeable plantsman. After many years at Gledhill Nursery in West Hartford, in 1984 he started O'Brien Landscaping, which has evolved into O'Brien Nurserymen. He is an active member of several hosta societies, as well as the American conifer, hardy plant, maple, daphne, and rhododendron societies.

The extensive display gardens feature more than 1,600 different hosta varieties, as well as other shady characters including asarums, epimediums, woodland peonies, primroses, toad lilies and spring ephemerals. Since hosta plants change in appearance from the time you buy them to maturity, it is great to see full-grown specimens growing in the display gardens. At any one time, you can choose from an overwhelming 1,100 hosta varieties for sale, as well as other choice shade perennials and daylilies.

Japanese maples are another special collection, with almost 100 varieties, from the pink variegated 'Geisha Gone Wild' to the golden 'Autumn Moon' and the amethyst 'Purple Ghost.' You will also find a wide variety of unusual dwarf conifers, daphnes, and other woodies, including dwarf ginkgos, about 25 umbrella pine hybrids, and variegated forms of many conifers.

O'Brien Nurserymen is open for retail sales on designated weekends from April through October. Check their website for the dates.

Elizabeth Park

1561 Asylum Ave., W. Hartford, CT 06117
(860) 231-9443
elizabethparkct.org

AREA: 101 acres

HOURS: Daily dawn–dusk

ADMISSION: Free, donations accepted

AMENITIES:

EVENTS: Garden tours, plant sales, garden lecture series, concerts

Opened to the public in 1897, Elizabeth Park was born of the American Park Movement, and is the home of America's oldest public rose garden.

The property was originally the farming estate of Charles Murray Pond and his wife, Elizabeth. A wealthy businessman and politician, he died in 1894 and bequeathed his entire estate to the City of Hartford for a public park. The estate consisted of 90 acres and a generous trust fund to purchase additional land, hire a park designer, and maintain the property. Pond requested that it be a botanical park and that it be named after Elizabeth, who was an avid gardener.

Swiss-born landscape architect Theodore Wirth was hired as park superintendent, and he worked with the firm of Frederick Law Olmstead to design the new park. As a result, Elizabeth Park mingles two types landscape design: European formality within the natural settings—winding roadways, sweeping vistas, and peripheral trees—that are a hallmark of Olmstead's work.

The centerpiece of Elizabeth Park is the formal rose garden, 2.5 acres in size with 475 beds and more than 15,000 rose bushes. The arches are in bloom from late June to early July and are just spectacular. Many of the other roses continue to bloom from early June to October.

If you visit in June, be sure to see the separate Heritage Rose Garden, one of the few in the country. Also known as Old Garden Roses, Heritage Roses—Albas, Bourbons, Centifolias, Damasks, Chinas, Gallicas, Hybrid Perpetuals, Moss, Noisettes, Portlands, and Teas—are extremely fragrant and bloom only once in June. Some of these varieties predate 1867. They are exhibited in raised beds that form a five-petalled rosette symbolizing a centifolia, or 100-petaled rose, which is the typical form of a heritage rose.

In addition to its rose gardens, Elizabeth Park has several other notable areas. The Perennial Garden is formal in design, with a central wooden pavilion adorned with *Clematis jackmanii.* Enclosed by a hedge of dwarf Japanese yew, the garden features 1,600 perennials arranged in "cool" and "warm" color beds accented by silvery gray foliage. Each fall the Tulip and Annual Garden is planted with

11,000 tulip bulbs for a spectacular spring display. The Shade Garden features mixed plantings of herbs, perennials, ornamental grasses, woody shrubs, and small evergreen and deciduous trees. Several horticultural groups design, plant, and maintain specialty gardens in the park, including those devoted to herbs, dahlias, and irises.

Dinosaur State Park

400 West St., Rocky Hill, CT 06067
(860) 529-5816
dinosaurstatepark.org

AREA: 80 acres

HOURS: Tues.–Sun. 9–4:30

ADMISSION: Grounds: free; museum: $6

AMENITIES:

EVENTS: Family-oriented activities throughout the year

Although not a garden in the traditional sense, Dinosaur State Park offers an eye-opening glimpse of plant species from the Jurassic era and an education about the evolution of plants. One of the largest dinosaur track sites in North America, the park opened in 1968, two years after 2,000 tracks were unearthed during excavation for a new state building. Beneath the museum's geodesic dome, you will get a bird's-eye view of the preserved Mesozoic floodplain covered with footprints that were made 200 million years ago by Dilophosaurus, one of the largest carnivores that roamed the continent.

Surrounding the Exhibit Center are two miles of nature trails and the Dinosaur State Park Arboretum. The Arboretum contains more than 250 species and cultivars of conifers and living representatives of plant families that appeared in the age of the dinosaurs.

When dinosaurs first became numerous in the late Triassic Period, nearly all of the major groups of vascular plants except the angiosperms (seed-bearing plants) were in existence. Conifers, palms, ferns, and treelike horsetails dominated the landscape. By the mid-Jurassic Period, conifers had become more diverse, with the evolution of many of trees that we recognize today. Archaeologists have found angiosperm pollen and leaves in fossils from 140 million years ago. Fossils from about 90 million years ago contain evidence of several modern families of flowering plants: laurel, magnolias, sycamores, box, and sweet shrub. By the end of the Cretaceous Period, many modern plant families coexisted with the last dinosaurs.

The trees are arranged in groupings throughout the property. Sycamores and magnolias line the entrance drive, and Japanese umbrella pines greet you at the entrance to the Exhibit Center. The Southeast Collection features plantings of bald cypress, black gum, willow oak, pawpaws, sweetbay magnolia, Carolina allspice, and a persimmon. Nearby are a giant sequoia, four Dawn Redwoods and a golden larch. Other unusual species include cedar-of-Lebanon, monkey puzzle tree, lacebark pine, Yezo spruce, weeping katsura, and Persian ironwood.

Dinosaur State Park runs many education-al programs for children. Making casts of the dinosaur footprints is a must, and is not restrict-ed to kids. Who wouldn't want a dinosaur track stepping-stone in the garden? See the website for materials to bring.

Harkness Memorial State Park

275 Great Neck Rd., Waterford, CT 06385
(860) 443-5725
ct.gov/deep

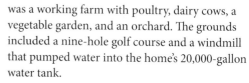

AREA: 220 acres total

HOURS: Grounds: daily 8 am–sunset; mansion: Memorial Day–Labor Day, weekends & holidays, call for hours

ADMISSION: Weekend/holiday parking fee

AMENITIES:

EVENTS: Annual Plant Sale in April; Harkness Day in September

With gorgeous views of Long Island Sound, Harkness Memorial State Park is a beautifully landscaped recreation area along the Connecticut shoreline. It was once the private summer home of the Harkness family, and boasts elegant gardens designed by Beatrix Farrand.

The focal point of the park is Eolia, a 42-room Roman Renaissance style mansion built in 1906, and purchased by Edward and Mary Harkness in 1907. It was named Eolia for the island home of Aeolus, keeper of the winds in Greek mythology. The Harknesses acquired their fortune through substantial investments in John D. Rockefeller's Standard Oil Company, and like many of the wealthy class during this period, they spent summers in the countryside.

Eolia was one of seven Harkness residences and the family's summer retreat. The 230-acre property was a working farm with poultry, dairy cows, a vegetable garden, and an orchard. The grounds included a nine-hole golf course and a windmill that pumped water into the home's 20,000-gallon water tank.

James Gamble Rogers created a grand walled garden with classical sculpture, an elevated wisteria-clad pergola overlooking Long Island Sound, tennis courts, and a lawn extending from a formal fountain court. In 1919 Beatrix Farrand remodeled the gardens. She converted the tennis court into the Oriental Garden—a special setting for the family's collection of Chinese and Korean vases and sculpture. Formal in layout, the garden featured a sunken grass panel and a central reflecting pool, and was planted with billowing flowers in soft pastels—baby's breath, dianthus, roses, lavender, and lilies—punctuated with heliotrope standards. Farrand revised the West Garden to a more naturalistic planting scheme, added a boxwood parterre surrounded by a whimsical wrought iron fence, and planted a sloping rock garden with alpine plants. Upon Farrand's retirement from practice in 1949, Marian Coffin updated the plantings in the East Garden. The gardens were faithfully restored to Farrand's and Coffin's plans by the Friends of Harkness in the 1990s.

The property includes the original farmhouse and servants' quarters, as well as the remains of the windmill and the Lord & Burnham greenhouse that once provided seedlings for the Harkness gardens and later for the State Capitol and other park facilities. Mature specimen trees and the remains of a cutting garden provide a glimpse of the property's bygone days. A stroll along the Niering Walk, a grass trail that winds through a native marsh, leads to Goshen Cove. A footpath from the imposing back lawn leads right down to the sandy beach.

Upon her death in 1950, Mary Harkness left the property to the State of Connecticut "for health purposes," with a third designated as a summer camp for handicapped groups and the remainder as a state park.

Florence Griswold Museum

96 Lyme St., Old Lyme, CT 06371
(860) 434-5542
florencegriswoldmuseum.org

AREA: 5 acres

HOURS: Tues.–Sat. 10–5, Sun. 1–5

ADMISSION: $10 adults

AMENITIES:

EVENTS: Garden Fest, changing art exhibits, children's programs

The Florence Griswold Museum is an extraordinary house, garden, and nationally-recognized center for American art and history. It portrays a period in the early 1900s when Florence Griswold's boardinghouse became a flourishing artist colony and America's center of Impressionist painting.

In the late 1890s Griswold, the youngest child of a once prosperous sea captain, found herself nearly 50 and alone in the world. She had outlived her parents and siblings and faced the future as an unmarried woman with few economic prospects. She had inherited one of the largest houses in Old Lyme—along with its debts. To survive, she took in boarders, which was a common and socially acceptable occupation for women at the time. In 1899 visiting painter Henry Ward Ranger fell in love with the house, the garden, and the view of the Lieutenant River. He established a Barbi-

zon-style art colony that lasted for 30 years and attracted more than 135 artists, including Childe Hassam, Willard Metcalf, Matilda Browne, and William Chadwick. Inspired by the beauty of the countryside and charmed by Griswold's hospitality, the Lyme Art Colony eventually became the center of Impressionism in America.

Miss Florence, as she was known, was a keen gardener and adorned her home with bouquets of fresh flowers from her garden. She was constantly in search of new and unusual plants and helped others, including the Lyme Colony artists, establish their own gardens. Griswold's garden was close to the house and designed in the Colonial Revival style, with rectangular planting beds overflowing with perennials, roses, and vegetables. Some of her favorites were hollyhocks, irises, foxgloves, heliotropes, phlox, cranesbill, rudbeckia, and daylilies. It was a visual feast for the artists, and became the subject of many paintings. In 2000 the museum's garden volunteers planted more than 1,500 heirloom perennials to restore the

garden to its 1910 appearance.

In 2006 the Museum completed restoration of the boardinghouse to its 1910 heyday, with recreations of an artist's parlor and Griswold's bedroom on the first floor. Of special interest is the dining room, with 43 scenes painted by the visiting artists directly on the wall and door panels. In addition to the house, the 13-acre site features a new 10,000-square-foot gallery, which hosts changing exhibitions of American art and culture. The Museum's extensive American art collection includes 890 paintings and nearly 2,000 works on paper spanning the 18th through 20th centuries. The site also includes the Rafal Landscape Center, a renovated barn with an exhibition illustrating a landscape's cultural importance; an education center; and the William Chadwick Studio, which serves as an example of a Lyme Art Colony artist studio.

Broken Arrow Nursery

13 Broken Arrow Rd., Hamden, CT 06518
(203) 288-1026
brokenarrownursery.com

AREA: 8 acres

HOURS: April–June: Mon.–Sat. 8–5:30, Sun. 10–4.
July–Oct.: Mon.–Sat. 8–4:30; Sun. 10–4

AMENITIES: 👥 👥

EVENTS: Grafting workshops, lectures

Broken Arrow Nursery is widely acknowledged in gardening circles as a source for rare plants. It has supplied trees for Martha Stewart's private garden, been featured on the Gardenista blog, and participated in specialty plant sales throughout New England.

Broken Arrow put down its first roots in 1947, when the young Dick Jaynes planted a couple hundred spruce seedlings in his father's apple orchard as part of a 4-H project. Those first trees led to a thriving Christmas tree farm on 20-some acres. His father kept it going while Dick was earning a doctorate in botany from Yale University.

In 1984 Dick and his wife, Sally, started the nursery. Building on his 25 years of research at the Connecticut Agricultural Experiment Station, they specialized in mountain laurel, the state flower of Connecticut. He is a world expert on mountain laurels, and you will find many wonderful cultivars at Broken Arrow.

In the past 20 years, the selection of plants offered at Broken Arrow has grown to more than 1,500, including both common and unusual woody plants and perennials. It is one of the few retail nurseries in Connecticut that propagates and grows most of the plants it sells. The nursery also continues to hybridize plants, and has developed new hybrids of Stewartia, witch hazel, winterberry holly, and other plants. Some of the unusual plants that you will find at Broken Arrow include the rosy kousa dogwood 'Summer Fun,' the beautiful Japanese maple 'Akika Nishiki,' the variegated ginger 'Jenkin's Jewel,' the variegated redbud 'Alley Cat,' the 'Miranda' hydrangea with gold and green foliage; a mayapple with square-shaped leaves called 'Goyoren,' and a cream-edged holly called 'Honey Jo.'

Twombly Nursery

163 Barn Hill Rd., Monroe, CT 06468
(203) 261-2133
www.twomblynursery.com

AREA: 7 acres

HOURS: Mon.–Fri. 9–5; Sat. 8–4; Sun. 9–4

EVENTS: Lectures

If you are looking for large specimens or unusual cultivars of trees and shrubs, visit Twombly Nursery in Monroe. It was founded in the 1960s by Ken Twombly, a plantsman, landscape designer, and garden writer known for his articles in *Fine Gardening* and other horticultural publications. He specialized in trees and shrubs and promoted designing gardens for winter interest. You can find one of his unique introductions for sale at the nursery, *Acer palmatum* 'Twombly's Red Sentinel,' a columnar Japanese maple with a unique, narrow upright shape—15' high and 8' wide at maturity—and burgundy foliage that turns a bright crimson in the fall. Twombly found it as a witch's broom (a natural mutation) on a 'Bloodgood' maple in a churchyard.

Andrew Brodtman and Barry Bonin bought the nursery in 2005 and grow spirea, Japanese maples, and dwarf conifers on three acres of growing fields. Since they have the land and resources, they harvest trees at 4" caliper or larger to provide gardeners with mature specimens of trees grown locally. Additionally, Brodtman visits growers in Oregon, Ohio, and the southern states every year to select rare and unusual plants that will delight his customers in Connecticut.

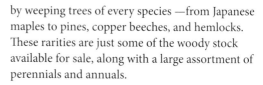

Hollandia Nurseries

103 Old Hawleyville Rd., Bethel, CT 06801
(203) 743-0267
ctgrown.com

AREA: 20 acres
HOURS: Daily 8–5
AMENITIES:
EVENTS: Annual spring flower show and fall festival

Owners Hans and Sally Reelick started Hollandia Nurseries in a small, two-car garage in 1964. Today the nursery is Fairfield County's largest garden center, with more than 20 acres of nursery space, mature display gardens, greenhouses, gazebos, and quaint shops.

The three acres of display beds at the front of the nursery are elegantly designed to showcase unusual trees and shrubs in a setting that is both a proving ground for the plant material and a source of inspiration for gardeners. A mixed border showcases a weeping Norway spruce with bright echinaceas and rudbeckias. A rock garden features an Asian lion statue guarding a prostrate blue spruce, variegated yucca, bright gold cypress, and a hardy cactus. A long grass allée is bordered by weeping trees of every species —from Japanese maples to pines, copper beeches, and hemlocks. These rarities are just some of the woody stock available for sale, along with a large assortment of perennials and annuals.

Hollandia hosts two annual community events. The Spring Flower Show includes a series of lectures, garden tours, representatives from major garden brands, and a season kick-off sale. The Fall Festival is a popular autumn celebration coupled with an exhibition of antique trucks, tractors, and other farm equipment.

After visiting the nursery, you can continue to Hollandia's Gift & Garden center to accessorize your garden with outdoor furniture, statuary, birdhouses, gifts, and decorations. It is located at 95 Stony Hill Rd. in Bethel.

The Elemental Garden

259 Main Street South, Woodbury, CT 06798
(203) 217-2464
theelementalgarden.com

HOURS: Mid-March–mid-August: Fri.–Sat. 11–5, Sun. 12–5, other days by appointment

AMENITIES:

The Elemental Garden offers one of the largest collections of garden antiques dating from the 18th through the 20th century. Owners Tracey Young and Dennis Kaylor travel to France and England several times a year in search of one-of-a-kind originals from grand estates and humble cottage gardens. Their aim is to provide the very best examples of classical garden ornament, from rustic to formal to mid-century modern.

To add elegant architectural detail to your garden, you can purchase French wrought iron garden gates, limestone finials, and English Victorian arbors. Historic garden ornaments include fountains, birdbaths, urns and planters, troughs, and statuary, all sporting a beautiful, weathered patina. Where else can you find late-19th-century terra cotta griffins from France and classic English hand-carved staddlestones? While the website provides ample information, it is well worth a drive to visit the shop in person and hear the colorful history of each piece.

Glebe House

49 Hollow Rd., Woodbury, CT 06798
(203) 263-2855
glebehousemuseum.org

AREA: 1 acre
HOURS: Garden: daily dawn–dusk; house: May–Oct.:
Wed.–Sun. 1–4
ADMISSION: $7; $2 garden only
AMENITIES: 🚻 🍴 ♿
EVENTS: Wine & Roses event, Colonial Fair & Muster in Sept.

Set in Woodbury's village center, Glebe House is considered the birthplace of the Episcopal Church in America, and offers visitors a glimpse of Revolutionary War-era Connecticut. The 18th century house portrays the home life of Reverend John Rutgers Marshall, his family of nine children, and their three slaves who lived in the "glebe" during the tumultuous years of the War for Independence. (The glebe was land which provided income for a clergyman and his family.)

In 1925 Glebe House became one of the first historic house museums in the country. A year later renowned English garden designer Gertrude Jekyll was enlisted to create an old-fashioned, English-style flower garden on the grounds. For unknown reasons, her garden plans were never implemented, but serendipitously the forgotten design resurfaced in 1978 among the papers of

Beatrix Farrand at the University of California, Berkeley, and work on the garden finally began in the late 1980s.

A group of volunteers completed the installation of the garden surrounding the Glebe House in the 1990s. It is the only Gertrude Jekyll garden in the United States. Jekyll never set foot on the Glebe property, but based her plans on photographs and written descriptions that were sent to her in England. The garden she designed for Glebe House garden includes a classic English-style mixed border, foundation plantings, a planted stone terrace, and a rose allée. She expected some changes would be made to the plan, based on the local climate and plant availability, and about 20% of the plantings, mostly woody evergreens, are substitutions for those in the original plan. Many of the perennials are older varieties. Annuals and biennials are also employed, as she would have used them to keep the garden interesting and colorful.

When you visit, enter the garden through the gate in the white picket fence at the front entrance to the house from Hollow Road. You will see the viburnum foundation plantings and 10-foot-deep perennial borders backed by evergreen hedges. On either side of the entrance are symmetrical plantings of lamb's ear, peonies, and bergenia. The 600-foot long border includes old-fashioned flowers—hollyhocks, peonies, iris, and dahlias. On the right of the stone path is the "cool" border, with waves of silver foliage and flowers in blues, whites, violets, and pale pinks. On the left of the path, the "hot" border sizzles with deep reds, oranges, and yellows. Jekyll preferred to plant in drifts rather than block-shaped patches, because, as she wrote, drifts do not leave "an unsightly empty space when the flowers are done."

On the east side of the house, a kitchen herb bed displays colonial culinary and medicinal plants. Further down the path is an allee of hydran-

geas, lilies and annuals, with a rose arch leading back to the cool garden beyond. The property is maintained by staff and volunteers who try to be faithful to Jekyll's plan, while presenting a garden of beauty in the 21st century. Miss Jekyll sits on a garden bench and supervises.

Hollister House Garden

300 Nettleton Hollow Rd., Washington, CT 06793
(860) 868-2200
hollisterhousegarden.org

AREA: 25 acres
HOURS: May–Sept.: Fri. 2–5, Sat. 10–4
ADMISSION: $5
AMENITIES:
EVENTS: Garden Study weekend in September

Hollister House Garden is modeled after classic English gardens such as Sissinghurst and Great Dixter—formal in its structure, but informal and a little wild in its style of planting. Overlooking the rolling hills of Litchfield County, the garden surrounds a rambling 18th century house set on 25 acres of beautiful wooded countryside with a winding brook and large pond.

Hollister House Garden is a 30-year labor of love for George Schoellkopf, who simultaneously ran a gallery of antiques and folk art in New York City, so the garden was a weekend hobby for many years. He created the garden to complement his historic house and outbuildings, with structural elements built from reclaimed stone, brick, and wood. Century-old granite curbing, salvaged from Hartford road renovations, forms terraces, wide stairs, and pathways that lead from one garden room to the next.

The terraced garden rooms are surrounded by tall walls and hedges, which offer inviting glimpses of the landscape beyond. Several 18th century barns and outbuildings are visible from the garden and reinforce the history of the place. Ponds, rills, and water troughs reflect the horticulture and sky. Elegant sundials provide focal points, while antique benches offer places to pause and enjoy the surrounding plantings.

The plantings in this garden are bold, surprising and artful. The flower beds are abundant with both common and exotic plants, arranged in captivating combinations. In the spring you will see extensive plantings of tulips, iris, and forget-me-nots, followed by old-fashioned roses, peonies, and vegetables in the summer. In late summer and early fall, lilies, dahlias, plume poppies, and Joe-Pye weed tower over shorter flowers. The brilliant autumn foliage of Japanese maples glows throughout. Gold and maroon varieties of many shrubs and trees provide a colorful backdrop from spring through fall.

Bunny Williams Garden

Falls Village, CT

AREA: 15 acres

HOURS: Visit through Garden Conservancy or Trade Secrets

Bunny Williams' private garden is open annually through the Garden Conservancy's Open Days and through tours sponsored by Trade Secrets (see box). Williams is a renowned interior designer and author of several books, including *An Affair with a House* and *On Garden Style*. Her 15-acre estate surrounds a historic New England manor and includes intensely planted garden spaces, beautiful ornamentation, and serene pastoral settings.

In the latest revision of *On Garden Style*, Williams invites the reader to rethink what a garden actually is. It is not just a perennial border, but the design of the entire space, including the overall style, hardscaping, furniture, ornaments, and containers. When you visit her private garden, you immediately see this concept displayed.

A long gravel drive lined with towering locusts and maples brings visitors to the front door. The house is bordered by several large flagstone patios that invite you to sit and relax in the lush green

Trade Secrets
Lion Rock Farm, Rte. 41 & Hosier Rd, Sharon, CT
tradesecrets.com
The annual fundraiser with a garden tour and sale of rare plants, garden antiques, textiles, and more was established by Bunny Williams. It is usually held in May—see the website for the date.

setting. The largest back terrace is designed as an outdoor room with comfortable sofas and chairs. Groupings of terracotta planters hold balls of boxwood and agapanthus. This patio looks out over a formal perennial garden adorned with evergreen hedges, topiary, and ornamental sculptures. Within this large garden, a rectangular koi pond surrounded by a flagstone terrace creates an intimate garden space. Beyond the perennial garden, a sculpted yew hedge frames an enclosed lawn.

From the guesthouse, Williams's visitors observe a formal parterre with neat rows of boxwoods laid out in diamonds and squares that surround colorful annuals and bulbs. Williams chooses a new color combination every year. Standard lilacs provide punctuation points in the space, and a rustic pergola at the far end is smothered with climbing roses.

Beyond the guesthouse, a board-and-batten barn overlooks immaculate vegetable and cutting gardens. Potted figs adorn some beds, while hand-forged iron tuteurs support climbing flowers and tomato vines. This garden is also bordered by a large greenhouse, where seedlings are started, newly purchased plants await their move to the garden, and tender plants spend the winter months. Next to the greenhouse is an ornate aviary with chickens and doves.

An uphill trail leads you from the formal spaces near the house to a looser woodland garden surrounding a pond. Primroses, epimediums, and trilliums bloom here in the spring, nestled among

ferns, hostas, and other shade plants. Past the pond, you will find a collonaded pool house that was inspired by a book on 18th century follies. Built with salvaged tree trunks, it evokes a classic Greek temple and is outfitted with wicker furnishings and simple unglazed terracotta. The pool house overlooks a limestone pool with French coping, and an old orchard planted with heirloom apple trees.

White Flower Farm

167 Litchfield Rd., Morris, CT 06763
(800) 503-9624
whiteflowerfarm.com

AREA: 10 acres
HOURS: April–Nov: Daily 9–4:30
ADMISSION: Free
AMENITIES: 👥 🛍️
EVENTS: Lectures and special events

White Flower Farm began in the 1940s as a second career for an enterprising young couple of writers—William Harris of *Fortune* magazine and his wife, Jane Grant, of *The New York Times*. They purchased a small barn in Litchfield and converted it into a country cottage where they could spend quiet weekends writing and exploring nature. They surrounded the house with a garden full of white flowering shrubs and perennials. Like other novices, they were soon under the spell of the garden.

Their shared hobby evolved into an all-consuming business. American gardening in the 1940s was ripe for new plants and ideas. Harris and Grant were happy to introduce new cultivars from Europe and Asia to U.S. consumers and to show them how to combine these plants into stunning gardens. Their nursery business grew until the

couple retired and sold it in the 1970s to Eliot Wadsworth. It remains a family run nursery to this day.

Set on a country road in bucolic Litchfield County, White Flower Farm is a wonderful destination nursery. With 10 acres of display gardens, there is something for everyone to admire. Are you a shade gardener? You will enjoy the tapestry shade borders of heucheras, ferns, hosta, Solomon's seal and coleus, anchored by gorgeous pots. Love begonias? The Begonia House features Blackmore & Langdon tuberous begonias from England in shades of red, salmon, orange, yellow, pink, and white. The famous Blackmore & Langdon delphiniums are new at White Flower Farm as well. Enjoy bulbs? White Flower Farm has some of the largest available, whether you are looking for amaryllis or Orienpet lilies. In fact, their lily sample packs are a great value. Are you a veggie gardener? You will find dozens of heirloom tomato varieties. Love hydrangeas? White Flower Farm always stocks the newest hybrids.

The most impressive feature at the farm is the perennial border, 280 feet long and 20 feet wide, bordered by a bluestone walkway that invites you to stroll and examine plant combinations. It's an American version of the late Christopher Lloyd's long border at Great Dixter, and was designed by Fergus Garrett, Lloyd's longtime gardener. Other sights to see: a curving tapestry hedge, 125 feet long, of five kinds of chamaecyparis that changes from green to gold to bronze; a grove of tree peonies; big pots of shade-loving annuals that can be ordered, pot and all, in the spring, and the Moon Garden, the namesake garden of all white flowers.

Bellamy-Ferriday House and Garden

9 Main Street North, Bethlehem, CT 06751
(203) 266-7596
ci.bethlehem.ct.us/bellamy_ferriday.htm

AREA: 104 acres

HOURS: May–Sept: Thurs.–Sun. 12–4; Oct.: Sat.–Sun. 12–4; open holiday Mondays

ADMISSION: $10

AMENITIES: 🏛 👥 🛍

EVENTS: Plant sale, guided tours

The Bellamy-Ferriday House and Garden embodies the dramatically different passions of two extraordinary individuals: Rev. Joseph Bellamy (1719–1790) and Caroline Ferriday (1902–1990). Rev. Bellamy was a renowned leader of the Great Awakening, the emotional religious revival of the 1740s. Completed in 1767, the house served several functions, providing Bellamy a place to live, to write famous treatises on religion, and to open the first theological school in North America. The 100-acre fully functioning farmstead with its numerous outbuildings remained in the Bellamy family until 1868.

The property went through several owners before it was purchased in 1912 by Caroline Ferriday's parents, Henry and Eliza Ferriday, as a summer

respite from New York City life. The couple updated the house with modern amenities and Eliza Ferriday began reshaping the outdoor spaces by designing a formal parterre garden and introducing a wide variety of fragrant trees, shrubs and perennials, sweeping lawns, and evergreens to provide privacy from the road.

The parterre garden is the centerpiece of the property. Eliza Ferriday was drawn to the Aubusson rug in the parlor and replicated its pattern for the formal garden. The parterre is rimmed with a clipped yew hedge, and features roses, peonies, and other perennials. The original roses were fragrant French roses, some with lineages traced to the 1500s, many of which ordinarily wouldn't survive the harsh New England winters. But careful siting inside the sheltering hedge allowed them to survive and thrive.

Following her mother's death in 1953, Caroline continued the stewardship of the estate. Bethlehem became her true home, and she began restoring the house to its original 18th century character. Under her care, the rose and lilac collections grew, and flowering shrubs were planted to soften the evergreen hedges. Specimen trees were also added, including a weeping hemlock, Franklinia, empress tree, copper beech, yellowwood, and a collection of magnolias. She also planted a weeping willow propagated from a tree on St.

Helena (Bonaparte's place of exile) as a symbol of her affection for Napoleon.

Caroline Ferriday was an actress, conservationist, civil rights advocate, philanthropist, and an ardent Francophile. She had lived in France during World War II, earning the Medal of France and the Cross of the Knight of the Legion of Honor for her work supporting the French resistance. After the war, she was instrumental in securing assistance for 35 Polish women who had been subjected to experimental operations in the Nazi concentration camp Ravensbruck. Her story became the subject of the *New York Times* bestseller *Lilac Girls*, written by Martha Hall Kelly in 2016.

Hill-Stead Museum

35 Mountain Rd., Farmington, CT 06032
(860) 677-4787
hillstead.org

AREA: 152 acres total, 1 acre cultivated garden
HOURS: Tues.–Sun. 10–4, house tours on the half-hour
ADMISSION: $15
AMENITIES:
EVENTS: Annual Poetry Festival, exhibits, First Sunday guided walks of grounds at 2:00 pm, sketching classes

With a historic house, lovely garden and impressive art collection, the Hill-Stead Museum and Garden is a fine example of a Country Place Estate from the early 1900s.

Hill-Stead was designed by Theodate Pope Riddle as a country home for her parents. She had grown up in Cleveland but was charmed by rural Connecticut when she attended Miss Porter's School in Farmington. She became the fourth registered female architect in the country, settled in Farmington, and designed Hill-Stead as a gracious Colonial Revival mansion that would showcase her father's antique furnishings and artwork. The 33,000-square-foot house was finished in 1901, and displays original paintings by Impressionists Mary Cassatt, Edgar Degas, Édouard Manet, Claude Monet, and James McNeill Whistler, as well as a print collection spanning 400 years.

Riddle was involved in many social causes including historical preservation, and became caretaker of the family's art collection. When she died in 1946, her will stipulated that Hill-Stead become a museum as a memorial to her parents and "for the benefit and enjoyment of the public." She called for the house and its contents to remain intact—not to be moved, lent, or sold.

The gardens at Hill-Stead were an integral part of Riddle's design for the property. She created an expansive Walking Garden of pathways that wove through informal plantings and created a transition between the house and the adjoining pastures and woodlands. She also designed a formal octagonal Sunken Garden for her mother, complete with a summer house, brick walkways, and a stone sundial. In 1920, Riddle hired Beatrix Farrand to update the Sunken Garden plantings, but there is no evidence that Farrand's design was ever implemented. With labor scarce during the war, Riddle had to grass over the garden, and after her death in 1946 it lay hidden and forgotten.

In 1984 the Connecticut Valley and Hartford garden clubs decided to resurrect the garden and discovered Farrand's original plans. They laid out the garden according to Farrand's drawings, replaced deteriorated hedges, widened the brick walks, and

planted as many period plants as possible. More than 90 varieties of perennials in shades of pink, blue, purple, and white accented with silvery-gray foliage now echo the color palette of the Impressionist paintings in the house.

The Sunken Garden reopened in 1988 and is now a prime attraction for the museum. While the Walking Garden has not yet been restored, you can hike the three miles of trails around a scenic pond. In the summer, Hill-Stead also hosts the annual Sunken Garden Poetry Festival. In line with Riddle's love of poetry, the festival features workshops, readings by award-winning poets, and live musical performances.

Crickett Hill Garden

670 Walnut Hill Rd., Thomaston, CT 06787
(860) 283-1042
treepeony.com

AREA: 8 acres

HOURS: May 1–June 21: Tues.–Sun. 10–5

AMENITIES:

EVENTS: See website

Traveling on a nondescript country road in western Connecticut, you will be surprised to find a nursery with hundreds of peonies in bloom. Cricket Hill Garden is a family-owned retail and mail-order nursery specializing in peonies and edible plants.

Cricket Hill Garden was founded by Kasha and David Furman in 1989. He had always been fascinated by China, and earned a master's degree in Chinese history. Since peonies are much beloved in China, he naturally became fond of them, and, after much effort, he acquired some authentic tree peonies from China.

The couple transformed a rocky, wooded hillside into a six-acre peony display garden dubbed Peony Heaven. Some of the peonies in this display garden are now more than 25 years old and magnificent. The Furmans have trialed more than 500 different cultivars of tree, herbaceous, and intersectional (Itoh) hybrid peonies, and they propagate only those that possess outstanding hardiness, vigor, color, form, or fragrance.

The inspiration for the parasols perched atop their peony trees comes from Chinese peony festivals, but the parasols also serve a practical purpose. While peonies grow vigorously in full sun, the flowers are sensitive to strong sunlight. Placing umbrellas over the plants protects the delicate flowers from sun and rain.

In 2010, son Dan joined the business, and expanded the nursery's offerings with hardy fruit trees and berries for edible landscaping. You can now find organic Asian pears, pawpaws, quinces, persimmons, heirloom apples, and many berry varieties, all perfect for Northeast gardens.

New York

SUGGESTED DAILY ITINERARIES

Morning
Yaddo Garden, Saratoga Springs (1)
Lunch–Boca Bistro, Saratoga Springs
Margaret Roach Garden, Copake Falls (2)

Morning
Clermont, Germantown (3)
Lunch–Gaskins, Germantown
Blithewood (4) and Montgomery Place, (5)
Annandale-on-the-Hudson

Morning
Bellefield, Hyde Park (6)
Springwood, Hyde Park (7)
Lunch–Culinary Institute, Hyde Park
Vanderbilt Estate, Hyde Park (8)

Morning
Locust Grove, Poughkeepskie (11)
Adams Fairacre Farm, Poughkeepsie (10)
Lunch–Ice House on the Hudson, Poughkeepsie
Innisfree, Millbrook (9)

Morning
Boscobel, Garrison (13)
Lunch–Brasserie Le Bouchon, Cold Spring
Stonecrop, Cold Spring (12)

Morning
Kykuit, Pocantico Hills (14)
Lunch–Sweetgrass Grill, Tarrytown

All Day
New York Botanical Garden, Bronx (15)
Lunch–New York Botanical Garden Café

New York

Yaddo Garden

312 Union Ave., Saratoga Springs, NY 12866
(518) 584-0746
yaddo.org

AREA: 10 acres

HOURS: Daily dawn–dusk; closed on Travers Day

ADMISSION: Free

EVENTS: Guided tours on Sat., Sun., and Tues. at 11am mid-June–early September, $10. Private group tours by arrangement.

In 1881, financier, philanthropist, and art patron Spencer Trask and his wife Katrina, a writer, purchased a country estate in Saratoga Springs that their daughter Christina named "Yaddo." They built a 55-room Queen Anne Revival mansion and welcomed artists and writers to visit.

Spencer Trask gave the 10-acre garden to his wife in 1899. Although the Trasks consulted landscape architects and gardening references, the garden's ultimate design was theirs. The mansion's lower lawn features a large pool with fountains and marble statuary. A wrought-iron gate inscribed with the name Yaddo leads to the gardens, which

occupy two terraces divided by a 180-foot long rose-covered pergola, and feature beautiful fountains. The lower terrace, which includes the rose garden, is the more formal and reflects the Italian gardens the Trasks had seen abroad. Four oblong beds bloom with more than 300 roses each. East of the roses are Italian marble statues of the Four Seasons, and a statue of a youth, *Christalan* sculpted by William Ordway Partridge as a memorial to the Trask children. The sundial overlooking the garden is inscribed with the poem "Time Is" by the Trask's friend Henry Van Dyke.

The upper terrace is a woodland rock garden, a style that came into fashion in the late 19th century. This shade garden, with its 100-year-old pines, features pools made of dolomite stone that are connected by a water rill. A large pyramidal pile of stones in the upper pool has a single spray fountain that fills the garden with the sound of falling water. Colorful perennials surround the lower pond.

Left without immediate heirs by the premature deaths of all four of their children, the Trasks bequeathed their fortune and estate to the establishment of a residency program for artists. The Corporation of Yaddo was founded in 1900 with the intent of providing "rest and refreshment [for] authors, painters, sculptors, musicians, and other artists both men and women, few in number but chosen for their creative gifts." The estate has welcomed many notable artists and writers including Truman Capote, Aaron Copland, Langston Hughes, and Sylvia Plath. The Trasks also stipulated that the gardens should remain open to the public free of charge, as they were during their lifetime. The gardens are maintained by the Yaddo Gardens Association, a group of dedicated volunteers.

Margaret Roach Garden

Copake Falls, NY
awaytogarden.com

AREA: 2.3 acres

HOURS: Open through Garden Conservancy Open Days

Margaret Roach's private garden in Columbia County is open for touring several times each year through the Garden Conservancy's Open Days. (See gardenconservancy.org for dates.)

Former executive vice president and editorial director of Martha Stewart Omnimedia, Roach left that life in 2007 for one of organic gardening and writing. She launched a popular blog called "A Way to Garden," wrote several books, and hosts a weekly public radio program about gardening. For Roach, gardening is not a mere hobby. It is an intellectual pursuit as well as a life practice—a spiritual journey into larger questions of existence and a lens into science and nature.

Roach's property is a former orchard with a simple Victorian-era farmhouse and little outbuildings set on a rural farm road in Taconic State Park. Informal mixed borders, shrubberies, frog-filled water gardens and container groupings cover the steep two-and-one-third-acre hillside. The garden, nearing 30 years of age, reflects Roach's obsession

with plants, particularly those with striking foliage. She loves the contribution of big, colorful, and textural foliage to the garden, and she is particularly enamored with the color gold. You will see many vibrant juxtapositions of maroon and gold throughout her garden—crimson Japanese maples underplanted with golden sedums, purple lilacs combined with golden sumac, wine-colored heuchera sharing a bed with bright yellow euphorbia.

The garden is compelling all 365 days of the year. Situated in Zone 5B, where frost stays well into May and can return in late September, means that the structure of the garden—the hardscapes, trees, and shrubs—must be carefully designed for year-round interest. Golden conifers, a mature umbrella pine, masses of winterberry, and swaths of hellebores extend the garden's beauty well into winter.

Margaret is devoted to the health of the environment and adheres to strict organic practices. She gardens without chemicals—meaning no synthetic fertilizers, pesticides, fungicides, or herbicides—and maintains a huge compost pile that nourishes her plants. She grows much of her food in a simple vegetable garden of raised beds. Caring for the environment has its rewards—more than 60 kinds of birds, along with native frog and toad species and the occasional bear, call the garden home and keep Roach company in her country garden.

Clermont State Historic Site

1 Clermont Ave., Germantown, NY 12526
(518) 537-4240
parks.ny.gov/historic-sites/16/hunting.aspx

AREA: 500 acre estate

HOURS: Grounds: daily 8:30–sunset; house: April 13–Oct. 31, Wed.–Sun. 11–4

ADMISSION: Gardens: free; house $7

AMENITIES:

EVENTS: Heirloom plant sale in June, other events

Clermont was the Hudson River seat of New York's politically and socially prominent Livingston family. Seven generations left their imprint on the site's architecture, interiors, and landscape. The most renowned member of the family was Chancellor Robert R. Livingston, an active patriot during the Revolution. He was a member of the Committee of Five that drafted the Declaration of Independence, wrote the New York Constitution, and served as the nation's first Secretary for Foreign Affairs. After the war he administered the oath of office to George Washington, and led the negotiations for the Louisiana Purchase. He was also co-inventor of the first commercially viable steamboat.

The gardens and grounds at Clermont are in the process of being restored to the 1930s, when John and Alice Livingston were the last private owners of the estate. Alice arrived at Clermont as a bride in 1908 and developed four main gardens at the estate: the South Spring Garden, with its view of the Hudson River; the Upper Garden, which provided cut flowers for the house; the 60-by-30-foot walled flower garden with symmetrical parterres; and the wilderness garden with its fish pond. The formal walled garden was inspired by the family's six-year sojourn in Italy, providing cultural education for their daughters, Honoria and Janet. It contains a fine collection of hellebores, which were Livingston's favorite spring flowers. "It is a great event with us when they arrive, and usually I place the flowers with some sprigs of boxwood, floating in a turquoise bowl," Alice wrote in her journal. The adjoining wilderness garden was meant to

"I am such a sucker for spring. I took a short walk in the garden this week, and my heart went all a-flutter to see nodding snowdrops, the magnolias just starting to bloom, and the daffodils up in full force."
—Alice Livingston

contrast the formality of the walled garden.

The South Spring Garden has been converted back to lawn. The Upper Cutting Garden is planted with perennials and contains the remains of a greenhouse that had been used to grow vegetables, roses, and flowers. Peonies were favorite flowers for bouquets for the house, and many heirloom peonies remain. Livingston introduced her daughters to gardening early. She gave each a garden plot next to the cutting garden, and the garden shed became their playhouse. Both daughters became gardeners as adults.

In the late 1920s, Livingston increased Clermont's spring floral display by expanding the Lilac Walk, which had been originally planted in the early 1800s. She added dozens of traditional varieties and fancy French hybrids, as well as other flowering trees and shrubs. Early May is an excellent time to visit Clermont, when the scent of lilacs perfumes the air.

During World War II, Alice Livingston, then a widow, moved into the gardener's cottage, and lived there for the remainder of her life, tending her beloved gardens. In 1962 the house and property were transferred to the State of New York. In addition to the gardens, Clermont's trails feature some of the best bird watching in the region.

Blithewood

Campus Road, Annandale-on-the-Hudson, NY 12504
845-752-5323
bard.edu/arboretum/gardens/blithewood/

AREA: 0.5 acre garden
HOURS: Grounds: daily dawn–dusk
ADMISSION: Free
AMENITIES:

Blithewood features a formal Italianate walled garden on the main campus of Bard College in Annandale-on-Hudson. At just 15,000 square feet in size, it is an intimate garden within a grand setting—130 feet above the Hudson River overlooking a panorama of the Catskill Mountains.

The garden was constructed in 1903 for Captain Andrew Zabriskie, a real-estate tycoon and captain of the National Guard, to accompany his Georgian-style mansion. Francis Hoppin designed the elegant space in the Beaux-Arts style popular in the early 20th century. Wide marble steps lead from the mansion to a highly architectural sunken garden with gravel paths on geometric axes, symmetrical beds, a central water feature, statuary, and marble ornaments. The walls create a peaceful green room, and a copper-roofed gazebo flanked by two wisteria-covered pergolas frames a majestic view of the river.

Historically the garden had an evergreen hedge around the fountain basin, and plantings of lilacs, roses, iris, wisteria, peonies, and annuals. Today's plantings are inspired by the historic palette, but include contemporary plant choices as well: grasses, hydrangeas, hardy geraniums, clematis, and a wide range of other perennials. Bard College and the Garden Conservancy are collaborating on desperately needed repairs to the historic structures and hardscape. The garden will remain open during the restoration.

The lawn areas surrounding Blithewood Mansion offer gorgeous views, with picnic tables and lawn chairs that invite you to linger. The grounds contain many of the campus's most important and venerable tree specimens, including a former New York State Champion red maple that is estimated to be more than 300 years old. The entire 550-acre Bard campus is an arboretum landscaped with many small pocket gardens, each with its own theme: a woodland garden, Japanese garden, Elizabethan knot garden, meditation garden, and more. Self-guided walking tour brochures of the campus arboretum are available at the Bertlesmann Campus Center information desk, or you can download a printable version before you visit at inside.bard.edu/arboretum/visitors/. The Campus Center also has a snack bar and restrooms.

Montgomery Place

Campus Road, Annandale-on-the-Hudson, NY 12504
(845) 752-5000
bard.edu/montgomeryplace/

AREA: 380 acres

HOURS: Grounds: daily dawn-dusk

ADMISSION: Free

AMENITIES:

Purchased by Bard College in 2016, Montgomery Place was, for nearly two centuries, the summer retreat of the Livingston family, whose members were prominent in politics, the military, and in New York social circles. Renowned architects, landscape designers, and horticulturists created an elegant country estate sited on 434 acres of rolling lawns, woodlands, and gardens overlooking the Hudson River and the Catskill Mountains.

The gardens at Montgomery Place were shaped by four women of different generations, but today reflect the period between 1925 and 1945 and the influence of Violetta White Delafield. Her husband General John Ross Delafield inherited Montgomery Place in 1921, and Violetta saw the property's potential, and need, for new gardens. An accomplished horticulturalist and mycologist who studied with some of the key botany professors at the time, she published three scientific monographs, and several mushroom species were named after her. The late 19th century witnessed a surge of

women into the botanical field, particularly on the Coasts. She applied her scientific approach to Montgomery Place: she did an inventory of the flora and commissioned a census of native plants on the property. She also applied her passion and creativity to developing the gardens there.

In their plans for the landscape, the Delafields first concentrated on the gardens surrounding the mansion. They terraced the slope behind the house toward the river, and planted flowers along the terrace balustrades. They also installed a naturalistic pond surrounded by white dogwoods at the base of the slope to foreshorten the visual distance to the Hudson River. They restored the trails and carriage lanes, and planted unusual understory trees such as kousa dogwood, silverbell, and sourwood.

Violetta Delafield was deeply respectful of the historic landscape she had inherited, but she also had her own ideas and was influenced by Beatrix Farrand and other American landscape designers of the day. One of the trends at the time was to create ornamental pocket gardens—small discreet garden rooms organized around a specific theme or style. Pocket gardens allowed Delafield to create a variety of different gardens while maintaining the overall naturalistic style of the property. She

installed an elaborate alpine garden with a frog pond that later morphed into a "wild garden" and is glorious in spring with the blooms of trilliums, trout lilies, bloodroot, ferns, and thousands of bulbs. She also added the peaceful "green garden" with an elliptical reflecting pool enclosed by hemlocks and rhododendrons.

Delafield added a potting shed and greenhouse to start annuals and to grow cacti and other succulents. She redesigned an old rose garden near the potting shed, and planted each bed in a different color scheme. She also planted borders of the 'Livingston' rose that she had found in her predecessor's kitchen garden, as a tribute to her family (actually it is the rose 'Jacques Cartier'.) A Colonial Revival herb garden with a central sundial was added next to the rose garden. Except for the expansive vegetable and cutting gardens, Violetta's gardens exist today and are maintained by Bard College staff and a band of volunteers, some of whom have been working at the garden for more than 30 years.

Bellefield

4097 Albany Post Rd., Hyde Park, NY 12538
(845) 229-9115 x2023
beatrixfarrandgardenhydepark.org

AREA: 2 acres of gardens
HOURS: Daily 7 am–sunset
ADMISSION: Free
EVENTS: Gardening workshops, design lectures

Adjacent to the National Park Service building, the Bellefield garden is almost hidden from view on the grounds of the Franklin D. Roosevelt National Historic Site. The mansion was the former home of Thomas and Sarah Newbold, who hired Thomas's cousin Beatrix Farrand in 1912 to design their garden. Farrand designed a whole plan for the property, which included a series of three interconnected walled gardens descending from the elegant 18th century house, as well as a rose garden, a lilac and fruit-tree allée, a boxwood parterre, and a kitchen garden.

The Newbold family donated the property to the National Park Service in the 1970s, and over time the gardens disappeared due to neglect. In 1994 a volunteer group was formed to restore the walled gardens, which you can visit on the property today. Although the walls and bed outlines of the garden were still in place, most of the plantings, as well as the original planting plans, were long gone. The walls and gates were repaired and replaced using Farrand's original sketches, and the garden was replanted based on planting plans she had created for other properties.

The Bellefield gardens are unique for several reasons. Farrand employed an interesting perspective illusion by making each garden smaller than the one next to it. This makes the garden appear longer than it actually is. She created drawings for the ornamental wrought iron gates and designed the native stone walls.

Farrand's signature design technique was the use of color-themed borders in many of her gardens, and this scheme was adapted at Bellefield. The

flower beds are planted in four color schemes: pink, white, mauve/purple, and blush/cream/gray. Each border displays a beautiful progression of bloom through the growing season. To enhance the illusion of a long perspective, bright colors—pinks, blues, and purples—are featured in the beds closest to the house, while lighter colors—whites, creams, and silvers—are used at the far end of the garden.

The best time to see Bellefield is in the spring and early summer, when the bulbs and perennials are in peak flower. The garden has four quadrants. The pink border's peonies are survivors from the original garden, and are flanked by foxgloves, phlox, and poppies in spring, followed by astilbes and 'Stargazer' lilies in summer. The white border's spring blooms include daffodils, camassias (also original), tulips, columbines and cosmos, followed by actea, phlox, anemone, and hosta. The mauve/purple border is filled with early crocus, irises, phlox, verbena, sea lavender, and balloon flower. The blush/cream/gray border displays dramatic lilies, plume poppy, and acanthus, underplanted with lamb's ear, santolina, and artemisia. Planting plans and plant lists for the color-themed borders are available on the website. The stone walls are covered with wisteria, akebia, trumpet vine, and honeysuckle. While few of Farrand's gardens exist today, her designs are just as appealing now as they were a century ago.

Springwood Estate

114 Estates Ln., Hyde Park, NY 12538
(845) 229-9115
nps.gov/hofr/index.htm

AREA: 265 acres total, garden is about 0.5 acre
HOURS: Grounds: daily dawn–dusk; house: daily 9–5
ADMISSION: Grounds: free; entire estate: $18
AMENITIES: 🏛️ 🚻 👥
EVENTS: Holiday Open House, hikes, exhibits

Springwood was the beloved home of Franklin Delano Roosevelt, the 32nd President of the United States. It was his birthplace, a haven that he returned to as often as possible, his political headquarters where he entertained numerous dignitaries, and his burial place. The gardens and 265 acres of woodlands and meadows on the Hudson River were an integral part of Roosevelt's life and nurtured a life-long interest in nature and the environment.

The original estate, consisting of a 15-room house on one square mile of property, was bought by FDR's father, James Roosevelt, in 1866. Springwood was a working farm, with a large vegetable garden, fields producing corn and hay, and experimental forestry plantations. The roads connecting outbuildings and various landscape features on the estate were heavily tree-lined, creating dense canopies throughout.

When asked his profession, FDR—whose titles included Governor of New York, Assistant Secretary of the Navy, and President of the United States— would respond: "I am a tree grower." Visiting the Chicago World's Fair in 1893, the young Roosevelt was attracted to the exhibit of trees native to New York State. From that time on, he studied and practiced the arts of planting and transplanting, pruning, watering, and spacing trees. Between 1911 and Roosevelt's death in 1945, more than 400,000 trees were planted on the Springwood estate. As president, FDR was responsible for the planting of 3 billion trees in the United States— with hundreds of thousands of those creating shelter belts to prevent another Dust Bowl.

The Rose Garden and Home Garden were key features of Springwood, and were supervised by FDR's mother, Sara Roosevelt. FDR sited his Presidential Library so that he could view the Home Garden from his office window, and so he would pass through the Rose Garden on his way back to the house in the evening. These were active gardens that the Roosevelts enjoyed as part of their everyday life. The Rose Garden contains 30 beds of hybrid tea and shrub roses in shades of pink, red, and white. Franklin and Eleanor Roosevelt are buried there with a simple monument marking the gravesite. The garden also features herbaceous

beds artfully planted with historic peonies and summer annuals.

The Home Garden—a large fruit and vegetable garden—was central to the life of the family. In addition to vegetables, it contained 21 apple and pear trees, as well as an apiary that provided pollinators for the fruit trees and honey for the family. FDR was particularly fond of the strawberries. His children and grandchildren helped weed and harvest from the garden. In 1946 the Home Garden was paved over to make room for parking, but the National Park Service began restoring the two-acre garden in 2017. The new garden will be planted with the same produce that the Roosevelts enjoyed during their residency. Since FDR was

a big proponent of Victory Gardens, the Park Service also plans to establish a Victory Garden education program.

Vanderbilt Mansion

119 Vanderbilt Park Rd., Hyde Park, NY 12538
(845) 229-7770
nps.gov/vama/index.htm

AREA: 211 acres total, garden is about 3 acres
HOURS: Grounds: daily dawn–dusk; house: daily 9–5
ADMISSION: Grounds: free; house: $10
AMENITIES:
EVENTS: Holiday Open House, lectures, exhibits

In 1895 Cornelius Vanderbilt's grandson Frederick and his wife, Louise, bought the Hudson River estate known as Hyde Park to use as their spring and fall country estate. Frederick Vanderbilt was a quiet man, active in the business of directing 22 railroads, while Louise was a wealthy socialite. They built a Neoclassical Beaux Arts mansion furnished with European antiques, and outfitted with all the latest innovations: electricity, indoor plumbing, and central heating. The grounds included a pavilion, coach house, two new bridges over Crum Elbow Creek, a power station, boat docks, a railroad station, and extensive landscaping. The final cost totaled $2.25 million—about $60.5 million in today's dollars.

Hyde Park was a self-sustaining estate, providing food and flowers for the family's needs there and at their other homes. The grounds had been shaped by several previous owners with horticul-

tural interests. In the early 1800s, Dr. Samuel Bard planted exotic plants and trees in the European Picturesque style. The next owner, Dr. David Hosack, had a passion for botany and established the first formal gardens on the estate, as well as extensive greenhouses to hold his exotic plants. He also hired André Parmentier to design the landscape. Roads, bridges, and lawns were laid out to compliment natural features, while large areas were left wild. Today, much of Parmentier's original design remains and continues to be admired for its grace and beauty. In the late 1800s, owner Walter Langdon, Jr., laid out the formal gardens and built the gardener's cottage, tool house, and garden walls, which remain and are in use today.

A large, formal garden was common to most Gilded Age estates, and Frederick Vanderbilt, who had a horticulture degree from Yale University, established the Italian-style, terraced garden that we see today. The upper garden features formal beds, while the lower garden exhibits a mélange of curvilinear shapes—crescents, hearts, and circular beds, all planted with bright annuals. An esplanade of cherry trees leads to a walled perennial garden, which opens up to a long reflecting pool and a brick loggia decorated with the statue of an odalisque in mid-dance. The path continues to a two-tier rose garden with a charming summerhouse.

The Vanderbilts were part of a new wave of urban elite that moved to the Hudson River Valley to enjoy relaxed country living, the sporting life, farming, and outdoor recreation. Hyde Park saw lavish weekend parties with horseback riding, golf, tennis, and swimming, followed by formal dinners and dancing. When not hosting guests, the Vanderbilts strolled through the gardens and greenhouses twice daily and visited the farm.

After Frederick Vanderbilt's death in 1938, the federal government purchased the estate, thanks to the intervention of President Franklin Roosevelt. While the grounds, landscaping, and buildings were preserved, there were no funds to maintain the gardens, which suffered years of neglect. Today the landscape is restored to its 1930s appearance, thanks to the Frederick William Vanderbilt Garden Association—a group of volunteers who have worked tirelessly to bring the gardens to their former glory. The formal gardens were replanted with 3,200 perennials and 2,000 roses. An additional 6,500 annuals are planted every year. The restored gravel paths, shady arbors, ornate statues, and bubbling fountains give the visitor a glimpse of life in the Gilded Age.

Innisfree

362 Tyrrel Rd., Millbrook, NY 12545
(845) 677-8000
innisfreegarden.org

AREA: 150 acres

HOURS: May–Oct: Wed.–Fri. 10–4, Sat.–Sun. 11–5; open holiday Mondays

ADMISSION: $8

AMENITIES: 👥

EVENTS: Guided garden tours, wildflower walks

Innisfree garden is the result of a deep friendship and collaboration among three people: owners Walter and Marion Beck and landscape designer Lester Collins. In the late 1920s, artist Walter and his avid gardener wife, Marion, bought their country residence, which they named Innisfree, and began to study garden design and philosophy. Walter Beck discovered the work of eighth-century Chinese poet, painter, and gardener Wang Wei. Studying scroll paintings of Wang's famed garden, Walter was drawn to the carefully defined, inwardly focused gardens sited within a larger, naturalistic landscape that Wang created. Wang's technique influenced centuries of Chinese and Japanese garden design, and the gardens of Innisfree. Drawing on Wang's approach, the Becks created vignettes

in the garden, which Walter called "cup gardens," incorporating rocks from the site with trees and plantings. Unlike Wang Wei, the Becks focused more on individual compositions. Relating these to one another and to the landscape as a whole was the role of Lester Collins.

The Becks met Collins early in 1938 and began their creative collaboration. He spent several years in Asia, and was dean of Harvard's landscape architecture department before starting his own private practice. His study of Chinese and Japanese garden design jived perfectly with the Becks' aesthetic. In his 20-year association with the Becks, Collins was able to create a magical garden that brought the Becks' "cup gardens" into a unified whole.

Having no children, the Becks decided to endow a foundation for the "study of garden art at Innisfree" that would make it into a public garden. Collins became the estate's manager, orchestrated its transition to a public garden, and continued to design and expand the landscape according to his and the Becks' vision. As funds allowed, he cleared portions of the densely wooded site, carefully editing existing vegetation to leave magnificent trees and swaths of natives, such as blueberries, iris, and ferns. He created the first route around the lake; added new cup gardens; designed such memorable water features as the Mist, the Water Sculpture, the Air Spring, and the Fountain Jet; sculpted fanciful berms like those along the Entrance Drive, and added new plantings of native and Asian varieties to create a garden that is natural, unpretentious, and sustainable. His involvement with the garden continued for 55 years until his death in 1993. Today, the garden is run by the Innisfree Foundation.

Innisfree is unlike other gardens, in that it is a naturalistic stroll garden in which the hand of the designer is almost invisible. The design comes from the study of the natural site. The gardens

at Innisfree are based around the 40-acre lake framed by wooded hills and rocky cliffs. Rocks are an important element—from stone walls and staircases to single monolithic stones creating a strong vertical in the landscape. Most of the stones were collected on the property and carefully placed in their current location. Dramatic water features provide movement and energy within the garden. Innisfree is a unique combination of Asian and American aesthetics. It is a garden of quiet beauty, serenity, and contemplation.

Locust Grove

2683 South Rd., Poughkeepsie, NY 12601
(845) 454-4500
www.lgny.org

AREA: 200 acres total; 3 acres of gardens
HOURS: Grounds: daily 8–dusk; mansion: May 1–Oct. 31 daily 10–5
ADMISSION: Grounds: free; house: $11
AMENITIES:
EVENTS: Peony sales, special events

Locust Grove was shaped by two families—the Morses and the Youngs. The Italianate style villa was built in 1851 as a summer home for Samuel F. B. Morse. Although best known for inventing the telegraph and Morse code, Samuel Morse was an artist and lecturer at the National Academy of Design and an avid gardener. As an artist he was strongly influenced by romantic 19th century design, which advocated a painterly approach to the landscape, with natural groupings of plants and curving lines. Morse used the property's natural features to shape the drives and paths and to create views. Morse's legacy at Locust Grove includes the majestic old maples, beeches, ginkgos, and tulip poplars that frame vistas throughout the property. A museum pavilion exhibits Morse's artwork and early telegraph equipment.

William and Martha Young brought a new vision to Locust Grove when they purchased the estate in 1895. They acquired adjoining properties and built scenic carriage drives along the Hudson. Martha Young was an avid gardener, and was especially fond of flowers. She expanded the formal gardens near the house, laid out long, straight flower borders, and planted a large collection of peonies, which continue to thrive today.

Her gardens have been preserved and augmented with additional plants since Locust Grove opened

to the public in 1979. Where possible, old varieties of perennials are used. Lavender, rudbeckia, echinacea, and hydrangea have been added to create a long bloom season. Since annuals were popular in the early 1900s, they are planted in drifts of a single color combined with blocks of perennials and selected shrubs to create 'pictures' that are beautiful whether as a detail or as a 100-foot-long composition. The peonies create an amazing display in June, and a 75-foot-long border of dahlias adds color after the peonies have passed.

Near the house, the circular flower beds and urns are bedded out in Victorian style with tulips in spring, and annuals such as coleus, marigolds, ferns, and castor beans in the summer. The Heritage Vegetable Garden occupies the old kitchen garden's site and exhibits the fruits and vegetables that were grown on the estate. A group of dedicated volunteers maintains the gardens.

Adams Fairacre Farms

765 Dutchess Tpke., Poughkeepsie, NY 12603
(845) 454-4330
.adamsfarms.com

HOURS: Mon.–Fri. 8–9, Sat. 8–8, Sun. 8–7
AMENITIES:
EVENTS: Annual Lawn & Garden Show in Feb-March
OTHER LOCATIONS: Kingston, Newburgh, Wappinger

Adams Fairacre Farms illustrates a new concept in shopping for the home and garden. It is like a Whole Foods and a premium garden center combined under one roof—a place where you can spend your entire Saturday morning shopping for all that you need. Adams began in 1919 as a road-side farm stand in Poughkeepsie run by Ralph A. Adams and his family. Today, it continues as a family-owned and -operated business with four locations in the Hudson Valley, and a loyal follow-ing of customers.

On the site of the original Adams Farm, the family oversees five acres of greenhouses and a produc-

tion area where more than two million bedding plants are grown annually from seed, as well as 300,000 hardy perennials, 110,000 mums and 80,000 poinsettias. It's one of the most extensive selections of locally grown plants in the Hud-son Valley. Adams has confidence in their plant stock—they offer a two-year guarantee on all their trees and shrubs. They also carry a wide array of unusual conifers, Japanese maples, and land-scape-size trees of all types.

The indoor Garden Center offers everything from seeds and seed-starting accessories, to garden tools, bird food and houses, patio furniture, grills, and hydroponic supplies. A Tropical Greenhouse features houseplants, as well as seasonal deco-rations, flower baskets, and annuals. Each year in late February through mid-March, Adams hosts its own Annual Lawn & Garden Show. The landscaping crew designs and builds displays of walkways, ponds, and patios decorated with hundreds of flowering spring bulbs, annuals, trees and shrubs in the Adams greenhouses. Vendors, knowledgeable staff, and garden experts offer seminars, giveaways, and free raffles.

The original farm stand at Adams has been expanded into a mecca for foodies. In addition to reasonably priced fresh produce, there is a huge selection of prepared foods. Hosting a dinner par-ty? You won't find a larger collection of interna-tional favorites under one roof, from coffees, cured meats, cheeses, and fancy chocolates, to gourmet pastas and sauces. Need a gift? Stroll over to the gift shop. Tired of shopping? You can enjoy a cup of coffee or an ice cream cone at the Poughkeepsie café. A trip to Adams is a trip to the nursery that the whole family can enjoy.

Stonecrop

81 Stonecrop Ln., Cold Spring, NY 10516
(845) 265-2000
www.stonecrop.org

AREA: 60 acres

HOURS: April 1–Oct. 31: Mon.–Sat. 10–5, select Sundays

ADMISSION: $5

AMENITIES: 👥 🎫

EVENTS: Plant sale, tours, workshops

Stonecrop Gardens has become a destination for gardeners and students of landscape design since it opened to the public in 1992. Its founder was Frank Cabot, a financier and self-taught horticulturalist who began gardening to relieve the pressures of venture capitalism and ended up creating two of the most celebrated gardens in North America—Stonecrop in New York, and Les Quatre Vents in Quebec. He also founded the Garden Conservancy, and served as chairman of the New York Botanical Garden and advisor to botanic gardens in Brooklyn and Ontario.

Stonecrop began as a private garden in 1958, when Frank and his wife, Anne, built their home on 60 acres in the Hudson Highlands at an elevation of 1,100 feet. They began to garden on the rocky site and soon developed a passion for alpine plants. Since choice alpines were hard to come by, they started their own alpine mail-order nursery. Although the nursery no longer operates, you will see many alpines in Stonecrop's gardens and greenhouses, that available for sale.

Over the years the Cabots' garden grew to 12

acres. In the mid-1980s, they began planning for Stonecrop to become a public garden that would inspire and educate other gardeners. They engaged English horticulturist Caroline Burgess, who had studied at Kew Gardens and worked for Rosemary Verey. Under Burgess's direction, Stonecrop's gardens have expanded in scope and diversity and now contain an encyclopedic collection of plants.

A visit to Stonecrop is a serious immersion in plants and design ideas. Plan to spend several hours with a plant list in hand. Some of the high-lights include a cliff rock garden, woodland, and water gardens, an enclosed English-style flower garden, and systematic order beds representing over 50 plant families.

Inspiration may be found in all seasons, from the spring show of bulbs and the explosion of color on the cliff ledge, to summer's profusion in the flower garden and the subtleties of fall foliage and fruit in the woodland. There are also a 2,000-square-foot conservatory housing tender specimens, and display greenhouses of alpines, tropicals, and succulents.

Boscobel House and Gardens

1601 NY-9D, Garrison, NY 10524
(845) 265-3638
boscobel.org

AREA: 45 acres

HOURS: April 1–Oct 31: Wed.–Mon. 9:30–5. Nov. 1–Dec. 31: Wed.–Mon. 9:30–4

ADMISSION: Gardens $11; House, Garden & Exhibit $17

AMENITIES:

EVENTS: Hudson Valley Shakespeare Festival, art exhibitions

At the estate's opening celebration in 1961, New York Governor Nelson A. Rockefeller called Boscobel "one of the most beautiful homes ever built in America." A Federal style mansion with unique architectural features, columns, Palladian windows, and ornate exterior decorations, Boscobel had been slated for demolition just six years prior. Originally located 15 miles south in Montrose, the mansion was saved from the wrecking ball by a local grass-roots effort.

After the dramatic rescue, the mansion was dismantled and stored in various barns in the local area until a suitable site could be found. A year later the building was moved in pieces to a beautiful piece of land in Garrison and restoration began. The mansion is now open for tours and features one of the leading collections of furniture and

decorative arts from the Federal period, including fine pieces by Duncan Phyfe.

In 1959 Boscobel's benefactor, Lila Acheson Wallace, brought in the esteemed landscape architectural firm of Innocenti and Webel to create an appropriate historic setting for the newly-restored mansion. Although Boscobel had originally been sited on a working farm, Webel designed a landscape in the Beaux Arts and Neoclassical styles to complement the formal architecture of the house.

Within two years, the garden was completed. To give the feeling that the landscape had always been there, towering maples, weeping cheery trees, mature shrubs and an entire apple orchard were brought in on flatbeds and installed. A formal rose garden was planted, brick walkways were laid, and the entry driveway and forecourt were created in time for the public opening in May 1961. In the mid-1990s the grounds were expanded to include an additional 29 acres of woodlands—appropriate for an estate whose name comes from Bosco Bello—"pretty woodland." Winding trails lead through woods to an overlook with a rustic gazebo that offers one of the best views of the Hudson River.

Boscobel is a beautiful example of a romantic Beaux Arts garden. A large pond with a tall flume fountain welcomes visitors to the property. Next to the Visitor's Center, a sculpture garden honoring the painters of the 19th-century Hudson River School was installed in 2017. A grand allée of maples lines the drive to the forecourt of the house. Follow the brick path to the fragrant herb garden and continue through the heirloom apple orchard into the English-style rose garden. It features 150 varieties of roses represented by more than 600 bushes surrounding a classical fountain. Be sure to walk out to the Belvedere, which offers breathtaking views of the Hudson Highlands, Constitution Marsh, and the West Point Military Academy.

Kykuit

200 Lake Rd., Pocantico Hills, NY 10591
(914) 366-6900
hudsonvalley.org/historic-sites/kykuit

AREA: 249 acres

HOURS: May 1–Sept. 30: Thurs.–Sun. Oct: Daily except Tues. Nov. 1–13: Thurs.–Sun. ;see website for hours

ADMISSION: Tours $25 and up

AMENITIES:

EVENTS: Various tours offered

The Kykuit estate was home to four generations of the Rockefeller family and features a grand mansion, beautiful gardens, extraordinary art, and spectacular scenery. It has been meticulously maintained for more than 100 years, and is a site of the National Trust for Historic Preservation. Kykuit is accessible by formal tours only. There are four to choose from, ranging from 1.5 to 3 hours in length, depending on how much you would like to see of the mansion; the Coach Barn, with its collections of classic automobiles and horse-drawn carriages; and the gardens. Only the Landmark Tour and Grand Tour offer access to all of the gardens.

Kykuit, Dutch for "lookout" and pronounced "kei-kit", is situated on the highest point in the hamlet of Pocantico Hills, overlooking the Hudson River at Tappan Zee. It has a view of the New York

City skyline, 25 miles to the south. The imposing mansion, built of local stone and topped with the Rockefeller emblem, is located centrally in a 249-acre gated inner compound within the larger Rockefeller family estate.

The 40-room mansion was built in 1908 by John D. Rockefeller, founder of Standard Oil, and the richest man in America in his day. The initial plans for the property were developed by the company of Frederick Law Olmstead. Rockefeller was unhappy with their work, however, and assumed control of the design himself. He created several scenic winding roads and lookouts and transplanted mature trees to realize his vision.

In 1906, the oversight of the house and grounds was given to son John, who hired landscape architect William Welles Bosworth. Kykuit is considered Bosworth's best work in the United States. The design is loosely based on traditional Italian gardens, with strong axes, terraces, fountains, pavilions, and classical ornamentation. The terraced gardens include a Morning Garden, Grand Staircase, Japanese Garden, Italian Garden, Japanese-style brook, Japanese Teahouse, loggia, large Oceanus fountain, Temple of Aphrodite, and a semicircular rose garden. With stairways leading you from one level to the next, the garden invites movement and views.

John Rockefeller planned to use the house only in spring and fall, so trees were selected for their spring bloom, such as cherries and dogwoods, or for their autumn leaf color, such as the Japanese maples. Wisteria is one of the prevailing plants that ties the garden together—you first see it on the front façade of the house, and then it reappears on walls and pergolas throughout the garden. Fountains are another signature element, from the replica of a Boboli Gardens fountain with a 30-foot statue of Oceanus that greets you in the forecourt, to 39 other fountains that punctuate the

garden rooms. The inner garden has a Moorish theme, with a canal and a small fountain featuring a sculpted fountainhead and bronze swans. The gardens, which took over seven years to install, were completed in 1915, and exceeded their budget of $30,000 by one million dollars.

Governor Nelson Rockefeller, the last private owner of Kykuit, transformed its basement passages into a major private art gallery containing paintings by Picasso, Chagall, and Warhol, as well as extraordinary Picasso tapestries. Between 1935 and the late 1970s Governor Rockefeller added more than 120 works of abstract and modern sculpture to the gardens, including works by Picasso, Brancusi, Appel, Arp, Calder, Moore, and Giacometti. He precisely and skillfully sited the art to complement the classical formality of the garden and create stunning views. Their inclusion in the garden elevated it from a beautiful classic garden to an extraordinary experience of architecture, horticulture, and art.

New York Botanical Garden

2900 Southern Blvd., Bronx, NY 10458
(718) 817-8700
nybg.org

AREA: 250 acres
HOURS: Tues.–Sun. 10–6; open holiday Mondays
ADMISSION: $23 weekdays, $28 weekends
AMENITIES: 👫 👶 ✕ 🍼
EVENTS: Orchid Show, Daffodil Weekend, Plant Sale, Mother's Day Garden Party & much more

The New York Botanical Garden (NYBG) is a 250-acre living museum that showcases more than a million plants in extensive collections. It's also an educational center, open-air classroom, urban park, major arboretum, collection of display gardens, and a renowned research facility. It operates one of the world's largest plant-research and conservation programs, with nearly 200 staff members—including 80 Ph.D. scientists—working in its state-of-the-art molecular labs as well as in the field.

NYBG was founded by Nathaniel Lord Britton and his wife, Elizabeth—the 19th century's "power botany couple." He was a professor of botany and geology at Columbia University and an expert on plants of the Caribbean. One of the few women scientists of her time, she was a leading scholar of mosses and wildflowers. The couple visited Britain's Kew Gardens during their honeymoon in 1888, and proposed a botanic garden for their native state of New York shortly after. Nathaniel was the first director, a position he held for more than 30 years.

The Bronx site was selected for the botanical garden due to the beauty and diversity of its natural landscape. Notable architects and landscape designers collaborated to create the garden as it is today: Calvert Vaux designed the overall layout of the grounds, including the buildings and the elegant carriage routes that wind around rock outcrops, hills, dales, and forests. The Olmstead brothers formalized the master plan in the 1920s. Beatrix Farrand designed the rose garden. Marian Cruger Coffin laid out the ornamental conifer and lilac collections. Ellen Biddle Shipman created a long perennial border called the Ladies' Border. And T.H. Everett created the rock garden.

You can visit any month of the year—just make sure that you allow a whole day! NYBG has some of the largest plant collections in the world, including ones devoted to daffodils, azaleas, cherries, crabapples, magnolias, tree peonies, and herbaceous peonies, conifers, daylilies, and lotus.

The display gardens provide interest in all seasons. The 2.5-acre Rock Garden is an oasis of jewel-like alpine flowers nestled among its gravel beds, rocks, and crevices. A gently cascading waterfall and stream flow to a tranquil pond. In May the surrounding native dogwoods bloom with breath-taking swaths of tiarella, trilliums, and other spring wildflowers.

The Perennial Garden is stunning in spring with hundreds of tulips interplanted among bleeding hearts and other early spring perennials. Its four themed rooms contain distinctive collections of plants selected for their color or seasonality. Peak time is in summer when countless brilliant flowers bloom in waves of purple, pink, yellow, and red.

Penelope Hobhouse designed the Herb Garden. The evergreen boxwood parterre framework provides symmetry and structure for the soft beauty and fragrance of the herbs.

The Peggy Rockefeller Rose Garden is considered to be among the world's best rose collections. The triangular shaped garden was completed in 1988 and features more than 650 varieties of roses around a central gazebo.

The Lord and Burnham Conservatory is a remarkable example of Victorian-style glasshouse artistry. It is home to lush tropical rain forests, cactus-filled deserts, orchids, palms, aquatic and carnivorous plants, and seasonal displays.

New Jersey

SUGGESTED DAILY ITINERARIES

Morning
New Jersey Botanical Garden, Ringwood (1)
Lunch–DeNovo European Pub, Montclair
Van Vleck House & Gardens, Montclair (2)
Presby Memorial Iris Gardens, Montclair (3)

Morning
Greenwood Gardens, Short Hills (4)
Lunch–Marigold's, Summit
Reeves Reed Arboretum, Summit (5)

Morning
Frelinghuysen Arboretum, Morristown (6)
Lunch–Sette, Bernardsville
Cross Estate Gardens, Bernardsville (7)
Peony's Envy, Bernardsville (8)

Morning
Bamboo Brook, Far Hills (9)
Willowwood Arboretum, Far Hills (10)
Lunch--Gladstone Tavern, Gladstone
Leonard Buck Garden, Far Hills (11)

Morning
Deep Cut Gardens, Middletown (12)
RareFind Nursery, Jackson (13)
Lunch–Grounds for Sculpture, Hamilton
Grounds for Sculpture, Hamilton (14)

New Jersey

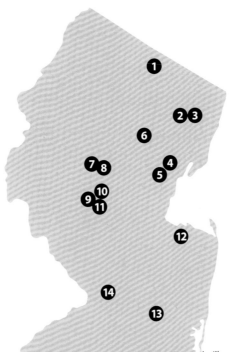

New Jersey Botanical Garden

Morris Rd., Ringwood, NJ 07456
(973) 962-9534
njbg.org

AREA: 96 acres

HOURS: Daily 8–8

ADMISSION: Free, parking $7 on weekends

AMENITIES:

EVENTS: Plant sale in May, manor tours on Sunday afternoons

The New Jersey Botanical Garden is part of Skylands, a historic estate in the Ramapo Mountains. Originally established by New York City lawyer Francis Lynde Stetson, the estate was sold to investment banker Clarence McKenzie Lewis in 1922. Both men were trustees of the New York Botanical Garden, and the property benefited from their care. Lewis transformed Skylands into a horticultural showplace. He removed Stetson's house and replaced it with a 45-room Tudor Manor House designed by John Russell Pope. The granite was quarried from the property, and many of the rooms contain antique paneling and stained glass, some of which date back to the 16th century.

To create Skylands's country-estate landscape,

Lewis hired the prominent firm of Vitale and Geiffert, and was actively involved in the project, stressing symmetry, color, texture, and fragrance in the gardens. He spent 30 years gathering plants locally and abroad and amassed one of the finest plant collections in New Jersey. In peak seasons he employed more than 60 gardeners.

In 1966 the State of New Jersey purchased the entire property, and the 96 acres surrounding the manor were designated as the state's official botanical garden. The elegantly landscaped grounds showcase more than 5,000 species of trees, shrubs, and flowers, and the specialty gardens provide something to see in all seasons. The east side of the manor house overlooks a series of five distinctive terraces. The first features the Octagonal Garden—an elevated rock garden with miniature alpine plants surrounding an octagonal pool. The second terrace is a fragrance garden, with a Magnolia Walk with sweetbay magnolias, viburnums, honeysuckles, and mahonias. This collection was situated near the house so that the scents would drift through the windows in June. In the third level's Azalea Garden, rhododendrons and double-flowering dogwoods surround a reflecting pool with a grotto, koi, and water lilies. Daylilies and annuals bloom in the fourth terrace's Summer Garden. And the fifth culminates in the Peony Garden with its Memory Bench; there, tree peonies bloom in May. Flanking the terrace gardens are the Pinetum and the Lilac Garden, which contains more than 100 lilac varieties, including French hybrids, Japanese tree lilacs, and Chinese lilacs that peak in mid-May.

On the west side of the manor, the Winter Garden displays colorful evergreens and stately trees, including New Jersey's largest Jeffery pine. Other notable trees flanking the manor include several magnificent copper beeches, a Japanese umbrella pine, an Algerian fir, an Atlas cedar indigenous to

North Africa, and the red oak that has stood in front of the library since the 1890s.

Crossing the road you will find yourself in the Annual Garden, which is anchored by a 16th century Italian marble wellhead, and the Perennial Garden, now restored to Lewis's original design. The Crab Apple Vista, an allée of 166 trees stretching a half mile, is a triumph of pink blossoms in early May. The Wildflower Garden features a beautiful display of Japanese primrose around its Bog Pond. Hosta collectors will appreciate the fenced Hosta/ Rhododendron Garden. The most unlikely of gardening sites is the Moraine Garden planted in the rock deposit left by Ice Age glaciers. Heathers, sedums, dwarf conifers, and ground-hugging alpines thrive in this ancient spot.

Van Vleck House and Gardens

21 Van Vleck St., Montclair, NJ 07042
(973) 744-4752
vanvleck.org

AREA: 6 acres
HOURS: Daily 9-6
ADMISSION: Free
AMENITIES: 🚻 ♿
EVENTS: Guided walks, lectures, workshops

Van Vleck House and Gardens provides an excellent example of the large homes built in this New York City suburb during the late 1800s. Three generations of the Van Vleck family lived on the six-acre property and designed the imposing and elegant dwellings and gardens.

Shortly after the railroad reached Montclair in the mid-1800s, mining and lumber executive Joseph Van Vleck moved his wife and 10 children from Brooklyn to this quiet suburb, where he built a family compound. The elegant Mediterranean-style villa that now graces the grounds was designed and built in 1916 by Joseph Van Vleck, Jr., who also created an Italianate green garden around the house. In 1939 his son, Howard, took up residence in the villa with his wife and four children. Like his father, Howard Van Vleck pursued a career in architecture and had a passion for the arts and horticulture. He left the professional field in 1930 to pursue his interests in painting and gardening full time, and redesigned the gardens to be more colorful and family-friendly. He enjoyed

hybridizing rhododendrons and strove to create a clear, yellow-flowering variety. A number of his hybrids survive as sentimental specimens in the garden, and several have been registered and named in memory of Van Vleck family members.

In 1993, Howard Van Vleck's heirs placed the property in the hands of The Montclair Foundation. This community foundation transformed the house into a center for nonprofits, but fortunately preserved the garden in its original state. A cell phone tour serves as a guide to the landscape. The most impressive feature of the garden is the enormous Chinese wisteria, planted in the 1930s. Although a vine, it has a trunk the girth of a mature tree. Circling the house's courtyard and winding up to the mansion's second floor, the wisteria is in its glory in mid-May.

The garden is sheltered from surrounding streets with plantings of mature conifers and broad-leaved evergreens that are also used to create separate garden rooms within. There are stunning collections of rhododendrons and azaleas, many of which Howard Van Vleck grew from cuttings. Formal lawns are bordered by long pergolas and walkways designed for strolling. Intimate garden nooks are furnished with benches. A wisteria-covered pergola overlooks the site of a former tennis court, which has been transformed into a classical garden with an iron urn fountain. The Formal Garden behind the house features beautifully planted perennial beds. The best time to visit this estate garden is in May, when the rhododendrons, azaleas, and magnolias are in full bloom.

At the back of the property, a former garage and the gardener's quarters with its adjoining greenhouse reference the separate houses they once served. Both were designed by Joseph Van Vleck, Jr, and serve as the Education and Visitor Center.

Presby Memorial Iris Gardens

474 Upper Mountain Ave., Montclair, NJ 07043
(973) 783-5974
presbyirisgardens.org

AREA: 8 acres

HOURS: Daily dawn–dusk

ADMISSION: Suggested donation $8

EVENTS: Plant sale Mother's Day weekend and following May weekends

Cultivated in New England since early colonial times, irises have a long and revered history. The Greek goddess Iris was the messenger of the gods and the personification of the rainbow. The fleur-de-lis is derived from the shape of the iris and is the symbol of the royal family of France. In Japan, the rhizome was ground to create the white face makeup for the geisha. And in New Jersey, irises are the stars of this memorial garden.

Frank H. Presby (1857–1924) was a leading citizen of Montclair and an iris hybridizer, collector, and founder of the American Iris Society. It was his expressed wish to give a collection of his favorite flower to Montclair's newly acquired Mountainside Park, however he passed away in 1924 before he could carry out his plan. The Presby Gardens were established thanks to local resident Barbara Walther, who led the effort and watched over the garden for 50 years.

Located at the base of the 7.5-acre Mountainside Park, the gardens were designed in 1927 by John C. Wister, a Harvard University landscape architect. He designed the garden in a bow shape, and Presby Gardens is now referred to as the "rainbow on the hill." The iris garden contains more than 10,000 irises of approximately 1,500 varieties, which produce more than 100,000 blooms over the course of the season. Peak bloom time is mid-May through the first week of June. Many of these irises were donated from Presby's and Wister's gardens, as well as from private Montclair gardens, the American Iris Society, and hybridizers all over the world.

Every iris in the garden has a marker indicating the name of the iris, the hybridizer, and the year the iris was registered with the American Iris Society. Twenty-six beds contain bearded irises, each dedicated to a particular decade. Be sure to look for the Heirloom Iris beds (beds 5a & 5b) with plants dating from the 16th to 20th century. Also look for the dwarf irises, growing only to 8 inches in height. They are the earliest of the bearded iris to bloom, and are ideal for rock gardens and fronts of borders.

Beds running along the creek bed contain a collection of non-bearded Spuria, Siberian, Japanese, and Louisiana irises, which prefer a wetter setting. Purple weeping beeches, fringe trees, katsuras, stewartias, redbuds, and ginkgos provide an interesting border for the iris gardens. A bee sanctuary with seven hives was added in 2000.

Greenwood Gardens

274 Old Short Hills Rd., Short Hills, NJ 07078
(973) 258-4026
greenwoodgardens.org

AREA: 28 acres

HOURS: May–Oct.: Thurs–Sun 10–5, select holidays

ADMISSION: $10

AMENITIES:

EVENTS: Bird walks, plant walks, twilight tours & more

Two very different American families left their marks on Greenwood Gardens. In the early 1900s, Joseph P. Day, a real estate auctioneer and self-made multi-millionaire, built the mansion and gardens as a retreat from hectic city life. Architect William Whetten Renwick designed both home and garden in an exuberant, heavily ornamented style. The garden was influenced by both Italian and Arts and Crafts styles, and laid out with strict axes and vistas. A series of lavishly planted terraces descended from the house, and an extensive system of paths made from exposed aggregate pavers led through lush, colorful plantings and recreational areas. The family could enjoy a croquet lawn, a tennis pavilion, a nine-hole golf course, a wading pool, shady pergolas and grottoes, a summerhouse, and a teahouse. The gardens were decorated with statuary and rough local stone embellished with colorful Rookwood tiles of the Arts and Crafts period.

In 1949 Peter P. Blanchard, Jr., purchased the property, and he and his wife, Adelaide Childs Frick, brought a more restrained classical formality to the estate. They replaced the flamboyant house with a Georgian brick mansion, and supplanted the extravagant flower beds with simple hedges of boxwood and yew and allées of London plane and spruce trees.

In 2000, following his father's wishes, Peter P. Blanchard III and his wife, Sofia, began restoring the garden to its early 1900s appearance and converted it to a nonprofit conservation organization with assistance from the Garden Conservancy. The garden needed extensive work. The walls, terraces, stairs, pools, statuary, and colonnades all had to be repaired. Trees and hedges were pruned or removed, and 28 acres of plantings were recreated from old photographs and notes under the direction of Louis Bauer, formerly of Wave Hill. After more than a decade of planning, fundraising, and restoration, the garden opened to the public in 2013.

Today's Greenwood Gardens illustrates a contemporary twist on classical planting. Long-lasting color is achieved with foliage, not just flowers. Gold 'Ogon' spirea softens deep green boxwood hedges, and feathery ferns envelope the stately columns of the Zodiac garden. Loose silver branches of Caryopteris 'White Mist' contrast with stiff yew hedges. The plantings complement the eclectic garden sculptures and ornaments. A towering, hand-wrought iron-grill gate, decorated with vines, ferns, parakeets, and birds of paradise, greets visitors in the parking area. Ceremonial granite hand-washing basins and whimsical oversized chess pieces frame the stone Tea House. Granite lanterns adorn the walls of the Cascade terrace, Chinese Fu dogs flank the stairs, and a bronze sculpture of a boy with two geese holds center stage in the Garden of the Gods. Phase Two

of the restoration will focus on the fountains and the dramatic Cascade—something to look forward to in future visits!

Reeves-Reed Arboretum

165 Hobart Ave., Summit, NJ 07901
(908) 273-8787
reeves-reedarboretum.org

AREA: 13 acres
HOURS: April 1–Oct. 31: daily 9–4; house open weekends
ADMISSION: Suggested donation $5
AMENITIES:
EVENTS: Annual wine tasting, daffodil day, maple sugaring fest; many educational programs

The Reeves-Reed Arboretum began as a country retreat called The Clearing and built by John Hornor Wisner in 1889. Wisner hired Calvert Vaux, a partner of Frederick Law Olmstead, to create an overall plan for the estate. Vaux designed a pastoral landscape that took advantage of the natural scenery and its views of the New York City skyline. The property's unique feature was "the bowl" a large, steep-sided depression created by a glacier more than 17,000 years ago. The Wisners sledded and skied in the bowl, and Isabella Wisner planted the first daffodil bulbs that are now a major Arboretum attraction.

In 1916, new owners Richard and Susie Graham Reeves transformed the gardens in line with the current fashion of landscape beautification. They replaced the kitchen garden and laundry yard with a series of formal gardens. Susie Reeves expanded

the daffodil collection with tens of thousands of bulbs, and commissioned landscape architects Ellen Biddle Shipman and Carl F. Pilat to refine the garden.

The resulting gardens are a beautifully maintained example of early 20th century landscape architecture. Elegant stone steps join the house to a landscape of themed garden rooms. Three of the gardens have been returned as closely as possible to their original appearance: the Azalea Garden, the Rose Garden, and the Rock Garden. During the Reeves' tenure, what is now called the Azalea Garden was simply the Flower Garden, planted with biennials and perennials in yellow, blue, and purple. It was the focal point of the property, where Susie Reeves spent much of her time and energy, and where her daughter was married in 1940. The bluestone borders in the lawn of the current Azalea Garden mark the outlines of the flowerbeds that were later abandoned due to the cost and labor of maintaining them.

The Rose Garden, installed around 1925, contains 286 rose bushes representing more than 150 varieties, including floribundas and hybrid teas, laid out in a traditional circle-in-a-square design around a cherub fountain. Susie Reeves exhibited her roses at the New Jersey Rose Show in nearby Morristown, where she was reportedly "showered with honors." Old-fashioned roses flank the formal garden, and climbing roses are trained on posts and chains. The adjacent Rock Garden with its pool and waterfall once featured sun-loving alpine plants. Now it is a shady retreat and an inviting habitat for birds.

In 1968, the Charles L. Reed family became the estate's last private owners, adding the patterned herb garden and opening woodland trails. In 1974 the Reeds joined local citizens and the City of Summit to preserve the estate as an arboretum

owned by the city. The Arboretum is a prime destination in April, when more than 30,000 daffodils bloom. After they fade, the bowl is a meadow for wildlife. A new two-level Perennial Border now overlooks the bowl, with epimedium, amsonia, anemones, alliums, and baptisia. An Island Garden in the parking area was planted with billowy plants in soft colors for late summer—grasses, agastache, perovskia, and caryopteris. Interesting specimens line the perimeter of the parking lot, including paperbark maple, Parrottia persica, and a large plum yew. The arboretum's fine tree collection includes katsura, sourwood, bald cypress, giant sequoia, and Franklinia trees, as well as a sugar maple, purple beech, and three ginkgos that are more than 100 years old.

Frelinghuysen Arboretum

353 E. Hanover Ave., Morristown, NJ 07960
(973) 326-7603
monmouthcountyparks.com

AREA: 127 acres

HOURS: Daily 8 am–sunset; Matilda's Café, April-Oct, Fri-Sun

ADMISSION: Grounds free

AMENITIES: 👥 🏛 ✖

EVENTS: Plant sale, flower shows

The Frelinghuysen Arboretum began as Whippany Farm, and was the country home of patent attorney George Griswold Frelinghuysen and his wife, Sara Ballantine Frelinghuysen, whose grandfather founded the Ballantine Brewing Company. The Frelinghuysens commissioned Boston architectural firm Rotch & Tilden to construct a summer home and carriage house on the property. The mansion, a fine example of Colonial Revival architecture, was built in 1891 and fashioned with Federal urns and swags, ionic columns on the porte cochere, and a large Palladian window on the second-floor landing.

The Frelinghuysens spent 40 summers at Whippany Farm and their winters in New York City. Their summer home was a working farm with greenhouses, barns, and outbuildings, and produced vegetables and flowers which were sent to the family in New York City via train.

Scottish landscape architect James McPherson designed the grounds in the style of an English country estate, with large trees, a Great Lawn, gazebo, knot garden, rock labyrinth, and a perennial and fountain garden. In 1920 Sara Frelinghuysen planted the formal Rose Garden, with beds laid out between the spokes of a Chippendale-style brick walkway set in a basket weave pattern.

The Frelinghuysens' daughter, Matilda, bequeathed the farm to Morris County in 1969. It was dedicated as the Frelinghuysen Arboretum in 1971 and put on the National Register of Historic Places in 1977. The formal gardens around the house were restored, with plantings of spring tulips and summer annuals. Trees in the park include willow, magnolia, bald cypress, beeches, crabapples, and flowering cherries. The park commission has added a series of educational demonstration gardens, such as color-themed gardens, shade and fern gardens, rock gardens, and raised gardens for people with special needs. There is also a special garden for plant collectors—the Promising Plants Garden of up-and-coming new varieties.

Cross Estate Gardens

61 Jockey Hollow Rd., Bernardsville, NJ 07924
(908) 766-1699
crossestategardens.org

AREA: 5 acres of gardens

HOURS: Daily 8 am–sunset

ADMISSION: Suggested donation $8

EVENTS: Plant sale in May. Garden tours Wednesdays from mid-April through October, 10 am

The Cross Estate Gardens date to the early 20th century when grand country mansions were built as summer retreats in the Mountain Colony of Bernardsville. Between 1903 and 1906, Ella and John Anderson Bensel assembled some 300 acres of property which they named Queen Anne Farm and built a 23-room stone house and outbuildings.

A civil engineer, Bensel was familiar with water systems. So it is no surprise that when he built his isolated summer villa, he added a water tower to make it self-sufficient. Capped with a wooden windmill, the five-story tower dominated the landscape and afforded scenic views of the countryside. Now restored, it once again provides water for the estate buildings and gardens.

In 1929, William Redmond Cross purchased the estate and renamed it Hardscrabble House. His wife, Julia Appleton Newbold Cross, was the daughter of Thomas and Sarah Newbold of Bellefield, whose garden had been designed by Beatrix Farrand. (See page 170). She would become president of the Horticultural Society of New York in the 1950s. With the help of landscape architects Clarence Fowler and Martha Brookes Hutcheson (a friend), Julia Cross made extensive improvements to the property and cultivated an unusual assortment of plants. She created a sunken walled parterre garden planted with annuals, and a natural garden of wildflowers planted in drifts among serpentine pathways. This pairing of formal gardens and woodland gardens was a favorite aspect of early 20th century landscape design.

In 1975, 162 acres of the property, including the primary buildings, were added to the Morristown National Historical Park. The addition provided assured protection for the adjacent 18th century New Jersey Brigade Revolutionary War encampment area. Funds were not available to maintain the gardens, which soon fell into disrepair, and in 1977 local residents began a volunteer project to revive them. Paths and walkways were uncovered and vegetation was removed, pruned, or replaced. Dedicated volunteers continue to meet at the garden every Wednesday from March to December. Their continued effort has preserved a fine example of an English country garden for others to enjoy.

Julia Cross's restored gardens are the star of the estate. The formal walled garden, created on two levels, features exciting combinations of perennials. May is an excellent time to see the tree peonies and the purple and white wisteria that adorns the stone pergola. In the neighboring wild garden, native shrubs and wildflowers are in bloom.

Peony's Envy

34 Autumn Hill Rd., Bernardsville, NJ 07924
(908) 578-3032
peonysenvy.com

HOURS: April 29–June 11: daily 11–5

ADMISSION: $10

AMENITIES:

If you're driving through New Jersey in the late spring, you must visit the world's largest public peony garden—Peony's Envy in Bernardsville.

Peony's Envy is home to more than 700 varieties of tree, herbaceous, and intersectional peonies that enjoy cult status among aficionados. The seven-acre production garden is also a beautiful display garden, with formal flower beds, stone walls, and meandering paths through the woodland.

The bloom sequence begins with the woodland and tree peonies, which open in early May. Many gardeners are unfamiliar with woodland peonies

(*Paeonia Japonica*) that prefer the early spring sun and summer shade of deciduous woodlands. These peonies sport delicate creamy white blooms in spring, lush summer foliage, and dramatic scarlet seedpods in fall. The 2,000 tree peonies at the nursery also prefer dappled sunlight, and produce dinner-plate-sized flowers. They are long-lasting woody shrubs from China and Tibet that can grow to seven feet. The nursery's herbaceous peonies bloom for a span of about four weeks, beginning with the fern leaf and coral varieties, followed by pink, white, and magenta. The last to bloom are the intersectional peonies—hybrids of tree and herbaceous peonies that come in many colors, including yellow.

During bloom season, each day the nursery receives more than 100 carloads of visitors. Owner Kathleen Gagan is welcoming and enthusiastic, and offers excellent advice to novice and experienced gardeners alike. If you miss the spring bloom season, Peony's Envy reopens again in the fall for bare-root sales, and peonies can be ordered via mail order from September to May. The nursery's extensive website is an excellent resource.

RareFind Nursery

957 Patterson Rd., Jackson, NJ 08527
(732) 833-0613
rarefindnursery.com

HOURS: Select weekends–see website for driving directions
AMENITIES:
EVENTS: Annual witch hazel festival, Build-a-Bog workshops, various events

"If you can find it in a garden center, we probably don't have it!" Hank Schannen said of the nursery he founded in 1998. Since that time, RareFind Nursery has stayed true to its mission, providing unusual and special plants.

Although he spent his career in marketing research, Schannen's passion was rhododendrons. He collected unusual varieties on the West Coast and in Europe, bred his own hybrids, and was an active member of the American Rhododendron Society. Schannen was fondly called "the Ambassador," a nickname that expressed his love and enthusiasm for the genus. Although he passed away in 2009, RareFind nursery continues to offer an impressive selection of rhododendrons and azaleas, including some of Schannen's hybrids.

RareFind operates primarily as a mail-order business, with an impressive following nationwide. The

nursery opens for retail sales on select weekends during the season and by appointment. Special collections you will find there are witch hazels, magnolias (including unusual yellow-flowered varieties), hydrangeas, and carnivorous and bog plants. RareFind also offers *Cornus kousa* 'Scarlet Fire,' a new deep pink dogwood introduction from Rutgers University that retains its bright color throughout the season.

RareFind is the only source for Liberty Trees, tulip trees that are direct descendants of the last standing Liberty Tree located in Annapolis, Maryland. During the American Revolution, patriots assembled under Liberty Trees for public meetings and protests. The British troops cut down most of these emblems of rebellion, but the 400-year old Annapolis tree survived until the hurricane of 1999. Seeds collected from it were used to grow the new generations of Liberty Trees sold at RareFind.

Bamboo Brook Outdoor Education Ctr.

11 Longview Rd., Far Hills, NJ 07931
(973) 326-7600
m66.siteground.biz/~morrispa/index.php/parks/bamboo-brook

AREA: 100 acres

HOURS: Daily 8 am–sunset

ADMISSION: Suggested donation $8

AMENITIES:

EVENTS: Various events through Park Commission; self-guided cell phone tour

Bamboo Brook Outdoor Education Center was once known as Merchiston Farm and was the home of landscape architect Martha Brookes Hutcheson and her husband from 1911 to 1959. Hutcheson was one of America's first female landscape architects and attended the School of Architecture and Planning at the Massachusetts Institute of Technology, along with Marion Coffin and Beatrix Farrand. Hutcheson's design for Merchiston Farm was completed shortly after the publication of her book *The Spirit of the Garden*, in 1923.

Hutcheson's European travels inspired her to design the garden in the Beaux-Arts style popular in the early 20th century. Drawing on European Renaissance and Baroque gardens as well as those of Islamic-era Spain, Beaux-Art gardens used formal geometry, allées and hedges, long vistas, reflecting pools and fountains, and native plants and materials. You see these design principles immediately when you enter the circular drive punctuated with white dogwoods underplanted with green hostas and white daffodils. Brookes used a restrained color palette and repeated the circle motif throughout her landscape.

The path from the driveway leads to the Upper Water—a pond designed to appear as a naturalized body of water. It was placed to take advantage of both the topography and the architecture of the house, and, importantly, it reflects the plants, the house, and the sky. A winding stream leads from the Upper Water to the rest of the garden. Hutcheson was fascinated with water features and constructed an intricate system of cisterns, pipes, swales, and catch basins to supply her house, pools, and gardens with collected rainwater.

The East Lawn and Coffee Terrace were designed with formal axial geometry. Informal plantings circle the oval East Lawn, which connects to the Circular Pool—a slightly sunken reflecting pool with six paths radiating from it and plantings of iris, phlox, ferns, dogwoods, and vinca. The Cir-

cular Pool was originally a farm pond in a natural hollow, which provided water for livestock.

Beyond the lawn lies an axial garden with a white cedar allée and parterres adjacent to a tennis court and the children's playhouse. Hutcheson placed rustic wood benches and chairs at spots where views could be enjoyed. She adapted native plants such as dogwood, lilac, sweet pepperbush, and elderberry to an Italian Renaissance-inspired design, and used native stone to create walls, patios, and steps throughout the garden.

The Little House was Hutcheson's quiet getaway. It was built over the small stream, which Hutcheson embellished with spillways and a lily pool, providing a home for water lovers such as sweetfern and iris.

A straight road lined with elms and oaks extends from the house to a farm complex including a farmhouse, barn, garage, and various work yards set in an informal landscape of fields and woods.

In 1972 Hutcheson's heirs gave the property to the Morris County Parks Commission, and it has been restored to its 1945 appearance. In addition to the

formal areas, there are numerous trails that wind through the fields and along Bamboo Brook, and connect to the Elizabeth D. Kay Environmental Center and Willowwood Arboretum.

Willowwood Arboretum

14 Longview Rd., Far Hills, NJ 07931
(908) 234-1815
willowwoodarboretum.org

AREA: 30 acres
HOURS: Daily 8 am–sunset
ADMISSION: Free
AMENITIES:
EVENTS: Lilac Party, lectures

The Willowwood Arboretum is a historic farmstead that became home to three extraordinary horticulturalists—brothers Robert and Henry Wells Tubbs and Professor Benjamin Blackburn. Today it houses the Willowwood Foundation, which is devoted to restoring and preserving the garden and educating the public about botany and environmental science.

The 135-acre farmstead was purchased in 1908 by the Tubbs brothers, enthusiastic gardeners who had professional careers in New York City. On the property were a farmhouse and several outbuildings. Massive willows lined a brook there, so they named it Willowwood Farm. The brothers' parents and sister joined them at the farm, and the entire family set to work. Ardent plant collectors, the Tubbs brothers developed relationships with renowned horticulturalists and plant hunters including Ernest Henry Wilson, Charles Sprague

Sargent, and their neighbor Martha Brookes Hutcheson. She introduced them to Professor Benjamin Blackburn, an instructor in Ornamental Horticulture at Rutgers and Drew University, who joined them in collecting plants and developing the gardens into a curated arboretum. Blackburn eventually became owner of Willowwood, and deeded it to the Morris County Park Commission upon his death in 1987.

You approach Willowwood on a long drive winding through the bucolic Long Meadow blooming with daffodils in the spring and wildflowers in summer. A wisteria-draped pergola welcomes you to a cluster of historic barns. Three formal gardens surround the Tubbs's house. The Cottage Garden, with its decorative wrought-iron gate, has colorful flower beds with perennials and spring bulbs on both sides of a stone pathway punctuated by slender cypresses. The back porch of the house offers views of Pan's Garden, with a bust of the Greek god Pan and a tapestry of plants in the pattern of a Persian prayer rug. The Mediterranean-style Rosary juxtaposes bold foliage and bright color. To the right of the house, towering bald cypresses and Japanese maples provide a shady retreat for an Asian-inspired garden with a woodland pool and waterfall.

The collector's spirit is evident throughout—from the orchards of flowering cherries and mature zelkovas, to the groves of lilacs, the giant Dawn Redwood, the numerous magnolias and viburnums, and the exotic conifers and trees with intriguing bark in the Winter Garden. Epimediums, hostas, tree peonies, orchids, and unusual perennials delight casual and sophisticated gardeners alike. Willowwood is a pleasure to visit in all seasons.

Leonard J. Buck Garden

11 Layton Rd., Far Hills, NJ 07931
(908) 234-2677
somersetcountyparks.org/parksfacilities/buck/LJBuck.html

AREA: 33 acres

HOURS: April–Nov.: Mon.–Fri. 10–4, Sat .10–5, Sun. 12–5

ADMISSION: Donation requested $3

AMENITIES:

The Leonard J. Buck Garden is one of the finest and largest rock gardens in the eastern United States. It consists of a series of alpine and woodland gardens situated in a 33-acre wooded stream valley. While most rock gardens are man-made and small in scale like the alpine plants they showcase, this rock garden is a series of huge natural rock outcroppings in a 500-foot-wide, 90-foot-deep gorge. The gorge was formed at the end of the Ice Age, about 12,000 years ago, when the water from melting glaciers carved out the valley of Moggy Hollow.

The rocky garden backbone was perfect for Leonard Buck, a geologist who made his fortune in mining. As he traveled the world on business, he collected rare plants. In the 1930s Buck was a trustee of the New York Botanical Garden, where he met and hired Swiss-born landscape architect Zenon Schreiber. Their goal was to develop a

naturalistic woodland garden composed of many smaller gardens, each with its own character and microhabitat.

Buck and Schreiber worked by eye and proportion, without a formal plan on paper. Buck worked the rock—chiseling, picking, and shoveling to expose the rugged face. Schreiber worked the plants, tucking in rare and exotic specimens and planting azaleas and rhododendrons at the base of the valley walls to create a dazzling display in spring. He also established a backbone of dogwoods, crabapples, shadbush, fothergilla, viburnums, and other native trees and shrubs throughout the property.

The garden's trails wind past two ponds and a rock-edged stream, through the woods, and up into the gorge. At its spring peak, the garden is a showcase for lady slippers, trilliums, woodland phlox, bergenia, iris cristata, tiarella, epimediums, and columbines. Siberian squill, Spanish bluebells, winter aconite, grape hyacinths, and other miniature bulbs enchance the floral display. Japanese primroses line the streambed and masses of azaleas dazzle in the valley. To help plan your visit, the website provides a weekly list of plants in bloom. There is something to see in every season.

When Interstate 287 was being laid out, the original plans called for the highway to run directly through Buck's property. However he invited the officials in charge to visit his garden and succeeded in having the interstate rerouted. After his death in 1976, the family donated the garden to the Somerset County Park Commission and set up a trust to fund maintenance and renovations.

Deep Cut Gardens

152 Red Hill Rd., Middletown, NJ 07748
(732) 671-6050
monmouthcountyparks.com

AREA: 54 acres

HOURS: Daily 8 am–dusk

ADMISSION: Free admission

AMENITIES:

EVENTS: Plant swaps, gardening programs

Deep Cut Gardens was named after the rivulet that makes its way through the sloped property. The gardens were established by mafioso Vito Genovese, who owned the property from 1935 to 1947. Genovese wanted a garden that would evoke his homeland of Naples, Italy. He hired landscape architect Theodore Stout to create "something big enough to make an impression from the top of the hill," and gave him free reign.

Since the original Colonial Revival mansion did not fully lend itself to an Italianate garden, Stout's design mixed English and Italian styles. The property had adequate water for the terraced water pools of traditional Italian gardens, so an elaborate rockery was constructed. Three cascading pools were encircled with volcanic rock that was allegedly imported from Italy at Genovese's request. These pools were dry and quiet for years, but have recently been refurbished. The sound of trickling water brings a delightfully cooling effect to this part of the garden. Ancient Sargent's weeping hemlocks form a shady green canopy over the cascading pools, which have been planted with ferns and other shade lovers.

Terraced gardens at the foot of the hillside are planted with heaths, heathers, and other rockery plants. Genovese's special requirement for the garden was a stone Vesuvius, complete with space for a fire inside the mountain's belly, and Stout filled the request on the left side of the hill. The rise provides a perfect vantage point to view the large, recessed parterre garden below. Surrounded by a low stone wall and anchored by a masonry pergola, the garden contains colorful roses and perennials.

Only two years after he purchased the property, Genovese left the United States to avoid arrest, and an unexplained fire destroyed his mansion. The property was eventually purchased by Karl and Marjorie Sperry Wihtol, who built the existing house and renovated the greenhouse and the gardens. In 1977 they donated Deep Cut Farm to the Monmouth County Park System to be used as a park and horticultural destination. The county began restoring the parterre in 2005. Years of design and preparation went into transforming the landscape to its 1930s appearance. The 180 rose bushes, perennials, and the surrounding boxwoods where planted in 2008.

Today, Deep Cut Gardens is dedicated to the home gardener. The 54 acres of gardens and greenhouses are a living catalog of cultivated and native plants to be observed through the seasons. To the historic gardens the county has added a butterfly and hummingbird garden, lily pond, shade garden, azalea and rhododendron walk, dried-flower production field, vegetable gardens, and the All-American Test Garden, which features new varieties of annuals, perennials and vegetables. In the spring, 1,400 tulips create a stunning display. Beyond the formal gardens, walking paths wind through the meadows and groves of chestnuts, oaks, maples, and ash, and around a natural pond. One of the site's year-round attractions is the 1,950-square-foot greenhouse Genovese installed, which showcases cacti, bonsai trees, orchids, succulents, and collections of tender plants.

Grounds for Sculpture

80 Sculptors Way, Hamilton, NJ 08619
(609) 586-0616
groundsforsculpture.org

AREA: 42 acres

HOURS: April–Dec.: Tues.–Sun. 10–6; Jan–March: Tues.–Sun. 10–5; timed tickets recommended

ADMISSION: $18 ($16 online)

AMENITIES: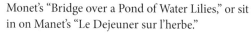

EVENTS: Curator walks, changing exhibits, art programs

Nestled in the heart of central New Jersey is Grounds For Sculpture, where art and nature come together to form a magical place. This open-air gallery garden exhibits more than 270 sculptures by renowned and emerging contemporary artists, each thoughtfully positioned within a meticulously landscaped park full of thousands of exotic trees and flowers.

The brainchild of prolific sculptor J. Seward Johnson, Grounds For Sculpture opened in 1992 on the former New Jersey State Fairgrounds outside Trenton. Johnson's desire was to make contemporary sculpture accessible to people from all backgrounds in an informal setting. His own iconic life-size bronze sculptures are found throughout the park—among them, his *Beyond the Frame* series based on Impressionist paintings. You can join Renoir's "Luncheon of the Boating Party," traverse

Monet's "Bridge over a Pond of Water Lilies," or sit in on Manet's "Le Dejeuner sur l'herbe."

The permanent collection at Grounds For Sculpture includes works by such distinguished artists as Clement Meadmore, Anthony Caro, Beverly Pepper, Kiki Smith, George Segal, Magdalena Abakanowicz, and Isaac Witkin. Special exhibitions of artists from all over the world supplement the permanent collection.

From the start, Grounds for Sculpture paid equal attention to artwork and site. The curator decides where to place the pieces, and a landscape architect and project manager work with the curator and the artist to determine how the work will look best and have the most impact. Hills, valleys, and waterways are created to support various sculptures. The resulting juxtaposition of art and nature provides an amazing aesthetic experience for the visitor.

The landscaping at Grounds for Sculpture incorporates more than 2,000 trees, as well as shrubs, perennial gardens, ponds, courtyards, terraces, and pergolas. Many of the plants were collected from estates, abandoned nurseries, and construction sites. You can walk through a bamboo forest, sit in a quiet enclosure, admire hundreds of lotus blooms in a pond, and walk through a wisteria-draped pergola. Everywhere you turn, delightful sculpted tableaus provide the sense that you are playing a role in the scene. Open areas display large sculptures that you can walk through. A surprise is around every corner, and most visitors walk through the gardens with smiles on their faces.

The fantasyland environment is fabulous for children. The majority of sculptures are touch friendly. Life-like sculptures, giant xylophones, tiny mazes, and tree tunnels form a natural playground, and dozens of peacocks wander the property. You can

spend a day here, enjoying the six indoor galleries, museum shop, and special programs, and have lunch at one of the two cafés, or dinner at the fine-dining option, Rat's Restaurant.

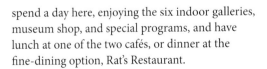

Pennsylvania

SUGGESTED DAILY ITINERARIES

Morning
Ambler Arboretum, Ambler (1)
Lunch–Magerk's Pub, Fort Washington
Highlands Mansion & Garden,
Fort Washington (2)

Morning
Meadowbrook Farm, Jenkintown (3)
Lunch–Flora Restaurant, Jenkintown
Hortulus Farm Garden & Nursery, Wrightstown (4)

Morning
Bartram's Garden, Philadelphia (5)
Lunch–White Dog Cafe, Philadelphia
Shofuso Japanese Garden, Philadelphia (6)
Wyck Garden, Philadelphia (7)

Morning
Scott Arboretum, Swarthmore (8)
Lunch–Terrain, Glen Mills
Terrain, Glen Mills (9)

All Day
Longwood Gardens, Kennett Square (10)
Lunch– Longwood Gardens Cafe, Kennett Sq.
Tea–Special Teas, Chadds Ford

Morning
Carolyn's Shade Gardens, Bryn Mawr (12)
Lunch–Minella's Diner, Wayne
Chanticleer, Wayne (11)
Tea–A Taste of Britain, Wayne

Pennsylvania

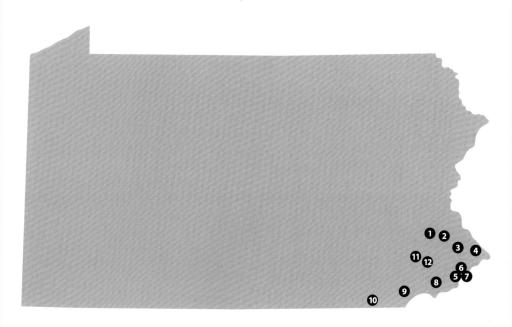

Ambler Arboretum

580 Meetinghouse Rd., Ambler, PA 19002
(267) 468-8000
ambler.temple.edu

AREA: 187 acre campus

HOURS: Daily dawn–dusk

ADMISSION: Free

AMENITIES:

EVENTS: Guided tours available, $5

The Ambler Arboretum of Temple University is a historic public garden that serves as a living laboratory for students of horticulture and environmental science. Its three areas of focus are sustainability, the health benefits of gardens, and the history of women in horticulture, agriculture, and design.

The Arboretum originated in 1910 with Jane Bowne Haines II, a descendant of the Wyck family of Germantown (see Wyck House, page 234). A graduate of Bryn Mawr College, Haines had toured Europe, visiting several colleges of gardening in England and Germany. When she returned home, she was determined to create a similar institution in the United States. With financial support from friends and fellow Bryn Mawr alumnae, she purchased a 71-acre farm near Ambler, where she founded the Pennsylvania School of Horticulture for Women. A colonial farmhouse on the property was renovated to provide offices, staff space, a

classroom, and dining hall, and in 1911, the school welcomed its first five students.

In the early 1900s women had few choices beyond marriage and family life, and the idea of educating them for careers in horticulture and agriculture was radical. The school played a unique role in both women's history and garden history. As the decades passed, enrollment remained small, but students went on to successful careers at institutions such as Longwood Gardens, Brooklyn Botanic Garden, Morris Arboretum, Colonial Williamsburg, and the National Arboretum. In 1958 the school became part of Temple University.

You can take a self-guided tour of the campus gardens, beginning with the Viola Anders Herb Garden, which was built by students and faculty in 1992 and displays a collection of culinary, dye, and medicinal herbs. The Arboretum's centerpiece is the Formal Perennial Garden, established in 1928. In May the long borders are ablaze with peonies, giant alliums, and baptisia. Twin gazebos surrounding a circular pond serve both as vantage points and focal points when the garden is viewed from the stairs of Dixon Hall.

Other gardens include the naturalistic Woodland Garden, with a lovely collection of spring-blooming bulbs, shrubs and trees. The Ground Cover Garden displays perennials suited for mass plantings. The Winter Garden features trees and shrubs with colorful branches, textured bark, and berries, underplanted with early-flowering bulbs. A conifer collection borders the greenhouses. The Healing Garden is designed around a central labyrinth. The Rain Garden starred as Temple's exhibit at the 2006 Philadelphia Flower Show. The Wetland Garden is an education in sustainable landscaping, with recycled-glass pavers, a biological filtration system for campus storm water runoff, a solar fountain, and plantings of natives.

Highlands Mansion and Gardens

7001 Sheaff Ln., Fort Washington, PA 19034
(215) 641-2687
highlandshistorical.org

AREA: 44 acres, 2 acre garden
HOURS: Daily dawn–dusk
ADMISSION: $5
AMENITIES:
EVENTS: Tours on weekdays at 1:30

Highlands Mansion and Gardens was home to three families during its 300-year history. The original owner was Anthony Morris, a wealthy politician and merchant who purchased 200-plus acres in Whitemarsh, Montgomery County, in 1794. There, he constructed an elaborate country estate named The Highlands to protect his family from the yellow fever epidemics sweeping Philadelphia. Morris suffered extreme financial difficulties and in 1808 was forced to sell The Highlands.

Philadelphia wine merchant George Sheaff bought the property in 1813, and his descendants owned it for more than a century. They created the two-acre "pleasure" garden east of the house, with its crenelated stone walls, formal perennial borders, grapery, and gardener's cottage. The noted 19th century architect and critic Andrew Jackson Downing described the garden as "one of the most remarkable in Pennsylvania," and in 1844 praised

The Highlands as "a striking example of science, skill, and taste applied to a country seat," noting that "there are few in the Union, taken as a whole, superior to it."

In 1917 socialite Caroline Sinkler, a native South Carolinian with ties to Philadelphia, purchased The Highlands and began extensive renovations to both the mansion and gardens. She created the current two-acre formal Colonial Revival garden, which earned a medal of excellence in 1933 from the Pennsylvania Horticultural Society. She also added stone walls, the exedra, and the greenhouse.

Walking through The Highlands can feel like a trip to Scotland. Long herbaceous borders culminate in a central fountain. A rose-covered pergola leads to boxwood-edged flower beds. Statuary and urns punctuate the landscape. An elegant herb parterre complements a Gothic Revival gardener's house. The aged stone walls are draped in grape ivy. Look for the ha-ha in front of the mansion, which was once used to keep farm animals in their pasture, and the exedra, which shapes a secret garden room.

Beyond the gardens, you can explore nine picturesque outbuildings, including a barn, springhouse, greenhouse, smokehouse, ice house, and tool shed. The Highlands Historical Society now owns the property, and has worked hard to restore the mansion and gardens to their historical beauty.

Hortulus Farm Garden and Nursery

60 Thompson Mill Rd., Wrightstown, PA 18940
(215) 598-0550
hortulusfarm.com

AREA: 100 acres total

HOURS: Nursery: May–Oct.: Mon.–Sat. 9–5, Sun. 9–3
Garden: May–Oct.: Tues.–Sat. 10–4

ADMISSION: Nursery is free; Self-guided garden tour is $15

AMENITIES: 🏛 👥 🚻

EVENTS: Founder-guided tours, museum tour, boxed lunch available

Hortulus Farm is a historic homestead amidst beautiful gardens and an accompanying nursery offering unusual tropicals, topiaries, standards, and begonias.

Owners Jack Staub and Renny Reynolds left their New York City careers when they acquired the 100-acre farmstead in 1980. Staub was a playwright and creative director in advertising, and Reynolds was a garden designer and event planner for celebrities. When they bought the property, they became gentleman farmers, garden designers, and writers.

At the heart of Hortulus Farm is the Isaiah Warner house, a classic Pennsylvania stone house built in the mid-1700s. It is flanked by two immense barns and rustic outbuildings that were added when

the farm operated as a large dairy. Meandering paths and gracious allées pass between ponds and over bridges, connecting more than 24 individual gardens. A woodland walk winds through native dogwoods, azaleas, woodland wildflowers, and more than 200,000 daffodils that welcome spring. Near the house are an elegant raised-bed potager and herb gardens. A pair of long perennial borders leads to the stunning pool garden.

Mature specimen trees, hedges, topiary, statuary, and follies enhance the garden, and Reynolds' retired party props are given new lives. An 18-foot-tall Eiffel Tower, which he found in England, made its U.S. debut at an "April in Paris Ball" at the Waldorf-Astoria. The carved white fence that encloses the kitchen garden once encircled the dance floor at Carnegie Hall's 90th-anniversary party. The white azaleas that carpet the woods once served as 1,600 centerpieces for a party at Rockefeller Center.

Visitors to Hortulus Farm are immediately impressed by the pastoral nature of the landscape, and the animals that call the farm home. Set among the formal gardens are dovecotes, an elegant cage with peacocks, and a chicken coop with a wisteria arbor. Horses graze in the surrounding pastures, and a large pond attracts ducks, swans, and a blue heron. Unlike many public gardens, Hortulus teems with farm animals and wildlife.

The Hortulus Farm Nursery offers lush tropicals, standards, topiaries, and unusual perennials, shrubs, and annuals. You will find interesting caged and frame-grown specimens—a favorite is the Plumbago 'Skyflower' grown on a 4-foot frame. There are abutilons and begonias, sedums, succulents, fuchsias, and pelargoniums that you will not find elsewhere.

Meadowbrook Farm

1633 Washington Ln., Jenkintown, PA 19046
(215) 887-5900
meadowbrookfarm.org

AREA: 25 acres
HOURS: Gardens: April–June: 10-5; July–Nov.: Wed–Sat.: 10–5, Sun. 10–3
ADMISSION: Free
AMENITIES: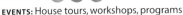
EVENTS: House tours, workshops, programs

Meadowbrook Farm is a destination nursery offering annuals, perennials, flowering baskets, trees, and shrubs—all set in a gorgeous Pennsylvania garden. It is the legacy of the late J. Liddon Pennock, Jr., a longtime prominent figure in the Delaware Valley's floral and horticultural design world.

Pennock came from a long line of florists, the first of whom arrived in Philadelphia in 1688 to garden on a land grant of a few thousand acres. Pennock took over the family business at age 20 and became florist to the Philadelphia elite, creating bou-quets for society weddings and centerpieces for debutante balls. Most notably he was appointed as the White House's floral director during the Nixon administration, decorating it for holidays, state visits, and Tricia Nixon's wedding. Pennock ran the Philadelphia Flower Show and was president of the Pennsylvania Horticultural Society.

Situated on 25 acres, Meadowbrook Farm was Pennock's home for 58 years. The two-story English Cotwolds-style house sits atop a hill, capturing dramatic views. The interior is exquisitely decorated and open for touring. Note the lizard figurines of all shapes and sizes throughout the home: they were gifts from friends due to his nickname, Lizard (a corruption of Liddon.)

Pennock created 15 intimate garden rooms on his terraced property. Many feature a fountain, statuary, pool, or gazebo from a past flower show, and most have a place to sit and enjoy the view. No more than 30 feet wide, the garden rooms are enclosed by stone walls or hedges. They intersect to create alleys that stretch hundreds of feet, creating the illusion of great space in just two acres of formal gardens. Each boasts a memorable name, such as the Eagle Garden, Dipping Pool, Woodland Path, or the fishpond called Loch Pennock. Meadowbrook's signature style is formal and rich

in detail, without being stuffy or overbearing. The gardens are planted with meticulously groomed trees, shrubs, and vines and accented with hundreds of annuals for seasonal color. Potted flowers, statues, architectural details, and furnishings decorate each area. Horticultural specimens are cleverly shaped, such as the espaliered magnolia on the terrace, or the yew in the front courtyard that is pruned into a cloud formation.

After retiring from the floral business in the early 1970s, Pennock opened a retail greenhouse specializing in tropicals and topiaries. When he passed away in 2003, he bequeathed Meadowbrook Farm to the Pennsylvania Horticultural Society, which has operated the property since. With a gift shop, greenhouses, and outdoor sales area, Meadowbrook Farm is full of ideas and whimsy. It's a one-stop destination for indoor and outdoor plants, exotic and rare specimens, and garden accessories.

Bartram's Garden

5400 Lindbergh Blvd., Philadelphia, PA 19143
(215) 729-5281
bartramsgarden.org

AREA: 45 acres

HOURS: Grounds: daily dawn–dusk; house: see website

ADMISSION: Free

AMENITIES: 👥 🚻

EVENTS: Guided tours Thurs.–Sun., Spring Plant Sale in May, Fall Plant Sale, Honey Festival

John Bartram was America's first botanist, plant explorer, and collector. He compiled a stunning selection of flora at his home garden and nursery from plant collecting expeditions across eastern America, as well as through his trades with European collectors. Located on the west bank of the Schuykill River, Bartram's Garden covers 45 acres. It includes his 1728 home and the historic botanical garden and arboretum that showcases North American plant species collected by three generations of Bartrams.

Bartram was a Quaker, a denomination that produced many naturalists at that time. He taught himself about plants through books and his own observations. His curiosity fueled a desire to collect plants from all over New England, as far south as Florida, and west to Lake Ontario. He collected seeds and plant specimens and established a relationship with another plant collector—London merchant Peter Collinson. Their plant swaps led to a burgeoning business. Prominent patrons and scholars in Britain were fascinated by the native American species, and were eager to purchase from Bartram's Garden. In 1765 King George III appointed Bartram Royal Botanist. At home in Philadelphia, Bartram received both George Washington and Thomas Jefferson.

Bartram's international plant trade and nursery business thrived under his descendants. Son William accompanied his father on most of his expeditions and became an important naturalist, author, and artist. William Bartram transformed the garden into an educational center that trained a new generation of botanists and explorers. Granddaughter Ann Bartram Carr built a successful nursery business that introduced Asian plants to the American public.

The Bartram garden has many distinct areas to explore. In front of the house is the Ann Bartram Carr garden, which celebrates her Asian plant introductions such as peonies and dahlias. Behind the house are the kitchen, flower, and medicinal plant gardens. And beyond those are woodlands of trees and shrubs that were collected, grown, and studied by the Bartrams from 1728 to 1850. These are primarily native plants of eastern North America: flame azaleas, highbush cranberry, Carolina allspice, sweetbay magnolia, and more. A bog garden illustrates the Bartrams' fascination with carnivorous plants. A separate area is devoted to plants William Bartram collected in the South, including bottlebrush buckeye and oakleaf hydrangea.

The garden also contains three especially notable trees:

Franklinia alatamaha: John and William Bartram discovered a small grove of these trees in October 1765 while camping by Georgia's Altamaha River.

George Washington visiting Bartram

William eventually brought seeds to the garden, where they were planted in 1777. The species, named in honor of John Bartram's friend Benjamin Franklin, was last seen in the wild in 1803. All Franklinia growing today are descended from those propagated and distributed by the Bartrams, who saved this tree from extinction.

Cladrastis kentukia (Yellowwood): A notably old tree, possibly collected by French plant explorer Andre Michaux in Tennessee and sent to William Bartram in 1796.

Ginkgo biloba: The Bartrams' is believed to be one of three original ginkgos introduced to the United States from China in 1785.

The property continues to the edge of the river, where there are opportunities for water recreation. Native plants and those discovered by the Bartram family are available for purchase year-round in the Welcome Center.

Shofuso Japanese House and Garden

Lansdowne Dr. & Horticultural Dr., Philadelphia, PA 19131
(215) 878-5097
japanesehouse.org

AREA: 1.2 acres

HOURS: April–Oct.: Wed.–Fri. 10–4, Sat.–Sun. 11–5

ADMISSION: $8

EVENTS: Japanese Culture celebration, monthly tea ceremony

Shofuso (Japanese for Pine Breeze Villa), is a traditional 17th century Japanese house and garden located in Philadelphia's Fairmount Park. This site has been the home of several previous Japanese structures and gardens, dating back to the 1876 Centennial Exposition.

Shofuso originated as a special exhibition entitled "House in the Garden" in the courtyard of the Museum of Modern Art in New York City. It was designed and built in Nagoya, Japan, using traditional techniques and materials, including Hinoki cypress wood. It was disassembled and brought to New York, where it was rebuilt and exhibited for two years, to rave reviews. Shofuso's garden at MoMA was designed by Tansai Sano, a Kyoto landscape architect whose family were caretakers of the famous dry garden in the Ryoan-ji temple for six generations. Eighty main stones were shipped from the old temple, which was located in central Japan.

When the house and garden were relocated to Philadelphia in 1958, they were situated in a Japanese garden designed in 1909. A waterfall and a new planting scheme were added. The property was further restored by a cadre of Japanese artisans in 1976, in preparation for the American Bicentennial celebration.

Three traditional types of Japanese gardens compose the 1.2-acre site: a hill-and-pond style garden which is intended to be viewed from the veranda; a tsubo-niwa, or courtyard garden, in the style of an urban 17th century Kyoto garden; and a roji, or tea garden, which is a rustic path to the tea house. In 2016 the *Journal of Japanese Gardening* ranked Shofuso third among 300 Japanese gardens in North America.

A majestic weeping cherry overlooks the house and pond. Visitors will enjoy the cherry blossoms in April, the azaleas in May, the colorful leaves of Japanese maples in the fall, and relaxing by the pond and feeding the giant koi year-round.

Wyck House

6026 Germantown Ave., Philadelphia, PA 19144
(215) 848-1690
wyck.org

AREA: 2.5 acres
HOURS: April–Nov.: Thurs.–Sat. 12–4
ADMISSION: Free
AMENITIES:
EVENTS: Rose Tours in June, Honey Festival in Sept. and many more programs

Wyck House is a haven for both history buffs and gardeners. As the ancestral home of the Wistar/Haines family for nine generations from 1690 to 1973, it illustrates the remarkable survival of historic Philadelphia life in a densely populated urban neighborhood. The 2.5-acre site includes the oldest rose garden in its original plan in America, perennial gardens, a woodlot, fruit trees, vegetable and herb gardens. The Colonial house is surrounded by a carriage house, greenhouse, icehouse, and smokehouse, and houses a collection of more than 10,000 family objects, pieces of furniture, and historical curiosities.

The Wyck's owners were Quakers, committed to innovation, social responsibility, and environmental sustainability. They became leaders in business, natural history, science, education reform, and

horticulture. Reuben Haines III (1786–1831) founded the Academy of Natural Sciences, the Franklin Institute, and the Pennsylvania Horticultural Society. Jane Bowne Haines II (1869–1937) was instrumental in the establishment of the Garden Club of America and founded the Pennsylvania School of Horticulture for Women, one of the first of such schools in the country. (See Ambler Arboretum, page 220)

The gardens at Wyck have remained largely intact since the 1820s and contain heirloom plants that have disappeared from other historic gardens. The largest tree in the garden is a native tulip poplar from the 1830s. A horse chestnut replaced the original Spanish chestnuts, which were wiped out by the chestnut blight of the early 20th century. The small pawpaw grove descends from native pawpaws grown on the property for at least 100 years.

The famous Rose Garden has changed little since Jane Bowen Haines I designed it in the 1820s. It is the oldest rose garden in its original plan in America, with more than 80 cultivars planted in parterres. The intimate garden retains its old-world charm, enclosed on one side by a wisteria arbor and on the other by a romantic garden shelter. (Legend has it that Wisteria is named after the Wistar family.) Wyck's historic roses are remark-

able for their beauty as well as for their fragrance, which fills the garden in June.

Also at Wyck is the Home Farm, with more than thirty beds of vegetables, annuals, perennials, and fruiting plants. A 1914 Lord & Burnham glass greenhouse is used for seed starting, several beehives produce honey, and hens lay eggs. Food grown on the farm is sold at an on-site farmers market.

Scott Arboretum

500 College Ave., Swarthmore, PA 19081
(610) 328-8025
scottarboretum.org

AREA: 300 acres
HOURS: Daily dawn–dusk
ADMISSION: Free
AMENITIES:
EVENTS: Plant sales, lectures

The Scott Arboretum encompasses the entire 350-acre campus of Swarthmore College, just seven miles from downtown Philadelphia. It is a series of gardens that showcase more than 4,000 different plants, and was established in 1929 in memory of alumnus Arthur Hoyt Scott. The combination of stately classical architecture and beautiful gardens makes Swarthmore College one of the most attractive college campuses in the United States.

There are 26 distinct garden areas within the Arboretum that can be seen on a self-guided tour lasting about two hours. The trees and shrubs have all been selected for their beauty, ease of maintenance, and resistance to pests and diseases. The

Arboretum is designed for interest in all seasons. In early spring, the Cherry Border displays 50 types of ornamental cherries suited to the Delaware Valley. More than 150 magnolias peak in the first two weeks of April, followed by lilacs, which formed the first Arboretum collection. In mid-May, you will enjoy the Rhododendron Display Garden. The Tree Peony Collection is also dazzling at this time, with more than 80 varieties, including Japanese and Chinese tree peonies, Itohs, French hybrids and Daphnis hybrids.

One hundred varieties of roses bloom in the Dean Bond Rose Garden from May through frost. Mid-summer is also the best time to enjoy the Theresa Lang Garden of Fragrance and the Pollinator Garden. The Hydrangea Collection steals the show in late summer, followed by the Metasequoia Allée and the Crum Woods in autumn. The Pinetum and Winter Garden are of special interest from November until March, with their striking conifers, winter jasmine, and swaths of hellebores.

Designed by Philadelphia landscape architect Thomas Sears and completed in 1942, the naturalistic outdoor amphitheater provides the backdrop for Swarthmore College's commencement ceremonies. Paths and stone steps wind through the native birch, oaks, and dogwoods of Crum Woods, opening onto the theater, which is built into a steep, natural slope. Screened by holly, oriental spruce, and red cedars, the 220-foot long amphitheater is edged by a low stone wall framed with mature rhododendrons. Eight curving retaining walls, each two feet tall and composed of native schist slabs, descend the 23-foot drop and create terraced, grass-covered seating. Sixteen mature tulip poplars and white oaks, spaced randomly, create a canopy above the audience.

For a listing of other college arboretums, see page 251.

Terrain

914 Baltimore Pike, Glen Mills, PA 19342
610-459-2400
shopterrain.com

HOURS: Daily 9–6
AMENITIES: 👥 🏠 ✖
Also at 561 Post Road East, Westport, CT

In 2008, the Anthropologie/Urban Outfitters team bought an 11-acre, 100-year-old garden center in Glen Mills, and transformed it into Terrain at Styer's, a garden destination aimed at the "light-hearted sophisticate"—a hip young customer. Terrain offers stylish home and garden accessories, indoor-outdoor furniture, and plants, which are displayed in chic indoor-outdoor environments, an onsite nursery, and a café. It's a place to meet a friend to browse for several hours and then enjoy a leisurely lunch.

Among the rustic wares on offer: willow edgers, stone topiary finials, Nutscene garden twine, handcrafted pottery, and a large assortment of vases, and terrariums. Orchids, succulents, topiaries, and tropicals are potted in handsome containers. All-natural soaps and creams are displayed on antique sideboards. Modern outdoor furniture, lighting, and seasonal decor are available for the discriminating shopper. The nursery yard displays native plants, annuals, and enough unusual varieties to satisfy the plant connoisseur. Everything is so well curated and elegantly staged that the store has become a wedding venue.

Carolyn's Shade Gardens

325 S. Roberts Rd., Bryn Mawr, PA 19010
carolynsshadegardens.com

AREA: 2 acres
HOURS: Select sale days–see website
AMENITIES: 🏛
EVENTS: Sale days

Carolyn Walker writes an informative illustrated blog called carolynsshadegardens and opens her home-based nursery to visitors for plant sales several times per year.

Although Walker comes from a family of notable gardeners, her first career was as an international corporate tax attorney. Gardening was a weekend hobby. In 1992, she decided she'd had enough of the corporate world. She began taking courses in horticulture and propagating her collection of shade plants.

One side of her property is dominated by large sycamores that lined an old carriage path. Beneath these graceful trees, Walker has created a woodland garden that is a living catalog of plants that are happy in the dappled shade. About 200 varieties of hosta, hellebore, pulmonaria, primrose, corydalis, hardy cyclamen, and heuchera grow there and are available for sale.

A self-described "galanthofile," Walker provides one of the few sources of unusual snowdrops in the U.S.; you can purchase them by mail order. The shade plants are available onsite during just four spring and two fall open houses and special sales.

Chanticleer

786 Church Rd., Wayne, PA 19087
(610) 687-4163
chanticleergarden.org

AREA: 48 acres

HOURS: April–Oct.: Wed.–Sun. 10–5. May–Labor Day: Fri. till 8 pm

ADMISSION: $10

AMENITIES:

EVENTS: Lectures, workshops, classes

Chanticleer has been called the most romantic, imaginative, and exciting public garden in America. This innovative 25-year-old public garden is one of 25 gardens featured in Tim Richardson's *Great Gardens of America*, and was named one of the "Top 10 North American Gardens Worth Traveling For" by the North American Garden Tourism Conference. Artistic, bold, and breathtaking, it has remained true to its founder's vision of being a "pleasure garden" for visitors young and old.

The Chanticleer estate dates from the early 20th century, when Philadelphians eager to escape the heat of the city built summer homes along the Main Line of the Pennsylvania Railroad. Adolph Rosengarten, whose pharmaceutical business became part of Merck, built his country retreat

in 1913. His son, Adolph Jr., began creating the magnificent garden when he came home from World War II. He had been stationed in Bletchley Park in England and fell in love with English estate gardens. Adolph Jr. and his wife, Janet, both enjoyed gardening, and maintained a huge vegetable garden, as well as flowers, shrubs and trees. He received an award from the American Horticultural Society as "one of the foremost gardeners in the country." When he left the property to the public following his death in 1990, the charter stipulated: "Operate the property as a beautiful public garden.… Educate amateur and professional gardeners."

Staying true to its original mission, Chanticleer has evolved into a horticultural triumph. While the original magnificent lawns, trees, historic buildings, and terraces remain, the staff added thematic garden rooms filled with creative plantings that are an inspiration to both professional and home gardeners.

The Teacup Garden is Chanticleer's courtyard—an intimate space anchored by a small Italianate fountain and planted with a seasonal display of plants. In the spring the fountain is surrounded by a lively combination of tulips, heucheras, burgundy lettuces, and herbs. In summer and fall, tropical succulents, bananas, pineapple lilies, and dozens of exuberant planters fill the small garden to overflowing.

What was once the old tennis court has been transformed into a bold flower garden. Planted with mostly bright-colored flowers, the palette changes from purples and yellows in spring to the reds and oranges of poppies, daylilies, and false sunflowers in summer.

The southwest-facing, sunbaked Gravel Garden is home to Mediterranean plants. In the spring this garden is graced with species tulips, miniature daffodils, and columbines. Come summer, orange

butterfly weed, lavender, Mexican feather grass, thyme, and yuccas explode in a tapestry on the hillside.

Beyond the slope, Bell's Run is a quiet respite surrounded by woodlands carpeted with grape hyacinths, trilliums, and primroses. The undulating lawn along the stream is a vision in blue when thousands of camassias bloom in the spring.

Planted with hundreds of azaleas, foam flowers, and ferns, Bell's Woodland celebrates plants of the eastern North American forest. You enter through a bridge sculpted to resemble a giant fallen beech tree that spans the creek. Wetland plants including skunk cabbage, rushes, and sedges line the creek bed.

The Ruin Garden, built on the site of Adolph Rosengarten, Jr.'s, residence, is composed of three theatrical rooms: a Great Hall with a fountain resembling a large sarcophagus resting on a mosaic "rug" of tile, slate, and granite; a "Library" of books sculpted out of stone; and a "Pool Room," where haunting marble faces gaze up from the depths of a grave-like water feature.

Throughout Chanticleer you will find handcrafted benches, chairs, metal railings, and decorations—the creations of employees who contribute not only their horticultural skills but also their artistic talents, including woodworking, stone carving, painting, and metalworking.

A favorite design element at Chanticleer are the decorative containers. Stocked with unusual plant combinations, these pots are works of art. Every year and every season bring a fresh scheme. It's worth returning several times a year just to see what's new in the pots!

Longwood Gardens

1001 Longwood Rd., Rte. 1, Kennett Square, PA 19348
(610) 388-1000
longwoodgardens.org

AREA: 1,077 acres total

HOURS: Sun. –Wed. 9–6, Thurs. –Sat. 9–10

ADMISSION: $23

AMENITIES:

EVENTS: Fountain Shows, music & theater performances, seasonal displays

One of the world's great gardens, Longwood has a history of legacy, innovation, and stewardship. Industrialist Pierre S. du Pont purchased the property in 1906 to save what was then the Pierce family arboretum from being sold for lumber.

Having grown up near Wilmington, Delaware, du Pont had a love for the area's natural beauty, and came from a long tradition of gardeners. He lost his father at the early age of 14, and became the father to his 9 brothers and sisters. After studying at the Massachusetts Institute of Technology, du Pont joined the family business, DuPont Company, a manufacturer of gunpowder, which had been started by his great-grandfather. Under Pierre's du Pont's leadership, the company expanded and diversified to become one of the largest corporations in the world.

When he bought the Pierce farm at the age of 36, du Pont had no great plan. He hired a landscape designer but was so disappointed with the results that he decided to design the gardens personally. He built the garden piece by piece, starting with a 600-foot old fashioned flower border of perennials, biennials, and annuals. Having traveled the world from an early age, du Pont was heavily influenced by the architectural qualities and water features of Italian villa and French chateaux gardens. He also was awed by the latest technology,

particularly the huge display of water pumps at the 1876 Centennial Exposition in Philadelphia, and the illuminated fountains at the 1893 World's Columbian Exposition in Chicago. He incorporated these features into his gardens, and spared little expense on the construction and mechanical costs of his massive conservatory and extensive system of fountains. Since he had no children, he founded the Longwood Foundation and left most of his estate "for the maintenance and improvement of the gardens."

You will need an entire day to see Longwood Gardens, and then you will want to come back again in a different month. In spring there are jaw-dropping displays of tulips, daffodils, and flowering trees. A highlight in summer are the 13 outdoor pools with massive water-platters and more than 100 types of tropical and hardy water lilies. In autumn, visit the famous Chrysanthemum Festival and enjoy the quiet beauty of the Meadow Garden with its grasses and native flowers. Winter at Longwood is marked with a magnificent indoor Christmas display, thousands of outdoor lights, and the topiary garden dusted with snow.

An interesting recent addition is the East Conservatory Plaza that is accessed with curved grass steps. Hidden beneath the Plaza is the Curving Green Wall with 47,000 plants (including 25 species of ferns) that create a vertical garden around 17 lavatory cabinets.

Longwood's greenhouses feature amazing displays throughout the seasons. The first was built to grow flowers, vegetables, and grapes. Du Pont created the 1921 Conservatory to showcase fruit and flowers in a decorative, horticultural way. The tradition continues today with dramatic seasonal floral displays.

Longwood Gardens is renowned for its fountains, which were an amazing feat of engineering when they were installed and continue to amaze visitors today. The five-acre Main Fountain Garden was reopened in 2017 after a $90-million, two-and-a half-year restoration. Hundred of fountains were refurbished, limestone embellishments and stone flowers were crafted by French masons in Wisconsin, and thousands of boxwoods were replanted along the gracious lawns. Set to music, the fountain shows are astonishing by day or night.

An amateur pianist, du Pont loved the performing arts. He constructed the world's largest residential organ for his ballroom and showcased the leading artists of his time. The tradition continues today with a year-round performance series of dance, theater, classical, jazz, and choral music.

Visiting Tips

GARDEN TOURING PACKING LIST

- ○ GPS

- ○ Maps

- ○ Phone/camera

- ○ Small notebook for recording ideas and plant names

- ○ Water and snacks: many places do not have dining options

- ○ Membership cards to gardening organizations. Some gardens participate in reciprocal admission programs.

- ○ Umbrella and rain gear

- ○ Sun glasses, hat and sunscreen

- ○ Sturdy walking shoes; waterproof shoes are best during morning visits

- ○ Trunk liner for unexpected plant purchases

GARDEN TOURING ETIQUETTE

Unlike public parks, gardens are designed for plant appreciation, not active recreation. Please use the following guidelines when visiting public or private gardens and nurseries:

* Smoking, fire and alcohol are generally not permitted on the premises.

* Leave pets, except service dogs, at home.

* Do not pick flowers, fruits, or plants.

* To protect the plant collections, active sports or games such as frisbee, bicycling, jogging, rollerblading, skating, ball-playing, and kites are generally not permitted in gardens.

* Do not walk in the flower beds, climb trees, or wade in ponds or water features.

* Deposit trash and recyclables in designated receptacles.

* Picnickers are usually welcome—check to see where tables are located.

* Silence your cell phones and leave radios at home. Consider your visit as an opportunity to escape from technological intrusions.

* Check in advance to see if organized gatherings and private events are permitted on the grounds.

* When photographing the garden, do not step into or place tripods in garden beds and respect the wishes of other visitors.

Eating and Shopping

BEST EATERIES

Briggs Nursery
Coastal Maine Botanical Gardens
Elizabeth Park
Florence Griswold Museum
Grounds for Sculpture
Longwood Gardens
Pickity Place
Sakonnet Winery
Terrain
Tower Hill Botanic Garden

BEST GIFT SHOPS

Briggs Nursery
Campo de'Fiori
Coastal Maine Botanical Gardens
Florence Griswold Museum
Garden in the Woods
Green Animals
Grounds for Sculpture
Longwood Gardens
New York Botanical Garden
Newport Mansions

Pickity Place
Strawberry Banke
Terrain
Tower Hill Botanic Garden
Vanderbilt Estate

WHERE TO BUY PLANTS

Adams Fairacre Farms
Avant Gardens
Bartram's Garden
Briggs Nursery
Broken Arrow Nursery
Campo de'Fiori
Carolyn's Shade Garden
Cider Hill Nursery
Cochato Nursery
Crickett Hill Garden
Garden in the Woods
Garden Vision
Heritage Museums & Gardens
Hollandia Nursery
Hortulus Farm
Kinney Azalea Gardens

Logee's
Longwood Gardens
Lyman Estate
Mason Hollow Nursery
Meadowbrook Farm
New York Botanic Garden
O'Brien Nurserymen
Peckham's Nursery
Peony's Envy
Pickity Place
RareFind Nursery
Snug Harbor Farm
Stonecrop
Sylvan Nursery
Terrain
The Farmer's Daughter
Tower Hill Botanic Garden
Trade Secrets
Tranquil Lake Nursery
Twombly Nursery
Walker Farm Dummerson
Weston Nurseries
White Flower Farm

Touring with Kids

Public gardens can provide a unique introduction to the beauty and variety of the plant world. Many public gardens feature children's gardens, provide activity backpacks, or host special family visiting days. Young children can be entertained with activity books, drawing supplies, and games—I Spy, Hide & Seek, and identification games. I found that when my kids were older, they enjoyed picnics, drawing, watercolor painting, photography, and looking for wildlife —birds, frogs, lizards, and fish—in the gardens. Binoculars and magnifying glasses were good accessories. A cooler of snacks and drinks was always a necessity.

BEST CHILDREN'S GARDENS

Coastal Maine Botanical Gardens
Berkshire Botanic Garden
Elm Bank
Heritage Museums & Gardens
Tower Hill Botanic Garden

Special Interest Gardens

EARLY SPRING GARDENS

Arnold Arboretum
Blithewold
Carolyn's Shade Garden
Chanticleer
Clermont
Garden in the Woods
Hortulus Farm
Leonard Buck Garden
Longwood Gardens
Mount Auburn Cemetery
New York Botanical Garden
Stonecrop
Willowwood Arboretum

EARLY AUTUMN GARDENS

Arnold Arboretum
Berkshire Botanic Garden
Chanticleer
Hollister House
Hortulus Farm
Kykuit

Longwood Gardens
Mount Auburn Cemetery
New York Botanical Garden
Stonecrop
Willowwood Arboretum

ROSE GARDENS

Arnold Arboretum
Berkshire Botanic Garden
Elizabeth Park
Fuller Gardens
Naumkeag
New York Botanical Garden
Roger Williams Park Botanical Center
Rosecliff
Roseland Cottage
Springwood
Swarthmore Arboretum
Vanderbilt Estate
Wyck Garden
Yaddo Garden

HERB GARDENS

Berkshire Botanic Garden
Elizabeth Park
Elm Bank
Glebe House
Hortulus Farm
Montgomery Place
New York Botanical Garden
Strawberry Banke

VEGETABLE GARDENS

Berkshire Botanic Garden
Bunny Williams Garden
Chanticleer
Elizabeth Park
Elm Bank
Longwood Gardens
Margaret Roach Garden
New York Botanical Garden
Stonecrop
Strawberry Banke
Tower Hill Botanic Garden

ALPINE GARDENS

Bedrock Gardens
Berkshire Botanic Garden
Chanticleer
The Fells
Leonard Buck Garden
New York Botanical Garden
Stonecrop
Tarbin Gardens
Tower Hill Botanic Garden

RHODODENDRON/AZALEA GARDENS

Heritage Museums & Gardens
Hortulus Farm
Leonard Buck Garden
Kinney Azalea Garden
Polly Hill Arboretum
Rare Find Nursery
Shofuso Japanese Garden
Van Vleck Garden
Weston Nurseries

HOSTA GARDENS

Carolyn's Shade Gardens
Cochato Nursery
Margaret Roach Garden
Mason Hollow Nursery
O'Brien Nurserymen
White Flower Farm

GREENHOUSES

Deep Cut Gardens
Logee's
Longwood Gardens
Lyman Estate
Pickity Place
Roger Williams Park Botanical Center
Tower Hill Botanic Garden
White Flower Farm

GARDENS WITH ART

Bedrock Gardens
Chesterwood
Cider Mill Gardens & Gallery

Florence Griswold House
Grounds for Sculpture
Highfield House
Hill-Stead Museum
Kykuit
Saint Gaudens Historic Site

GARDENS WITH HISTORIC HOMES TO TOUR

Bartram's Garden
Bellamy-Ferriday House
Blithewold
Boscobel
Chanticleer
Chesterwood
Clermont
Crane Estate
Eleanor Cabot Bradley Estate
Florence Griswold Museum
Fuller Gardens
Glebe House
Green Animals
Hamilton House
Harkness Memorial State Park
Highfield Hall & Gardens
Highlands Mansion & Garden
Hildene
Hill-Stead Museum
Kykuit
Locust Grove
Longfellow House and Garden
Lyman Estate
Meadowbrook Farm
Moffatt-Ladd House
Naumkeag
Nickels-Sortwell House
Ropes Mansion
Rosecliff
Roseland Cottage
Rundlet-May House
Saint Gaudens Historic Site
Sedgwick Long Hill
Shofuso Japanese Garden
Springwood
Stevens Coolidge Place

Strawberry Banke
The Breakers
The Elms
The Fells
The Mount
Vanderbilt Estate
Wyck Garden

COLLEGE ARBORETUMS

University of New Hampshire,
    Durham, NH
University of Southern Maine,
    Gorham, ME
University of Maine, Orono, ME
Colby College, Waterville, ME
Mount Holyoke College,
    S. Hadley, MA
Smith College, MA
University of Massachusetts,
    Amherst, MA
Wellesley College, Wellesley, MA
University of Rhode Island,
    Kingston, RI
Connecticut College,
    New London, CT
University of Connecticut, Storrs, CT
Yale University, New Haven, CT
Bard College,
    Annandale-on-the-Hudson, NY
Hofstra University, Hempstead, NY
Rutgers University,
    New Brunswick, NJ
Temple University, Ambler, PA
Bryn Mawr, Bryn Mawr, PA
Haverford College, Haverford, PA
University of Pennsylvania,
    Philadelphia, PA

Get Involved!

Gardening organizations, horticultural societies, and garden clubs are excellent resources for the garden tourist and offer regional tours of gardens that may not be normally accessible to the public. Some of these organization also offer nursery discounts and reciprocal admissions at other gardens.

GARDENING ORGANIZATIONS

Garden Conservancy
gardenconservancy.org

The Garden Conservancy was founded in 1989 by Frank Cabot to preserve and share America's most extraordinary private gardens. To date, the organization has helped preserve more than 90 gardens nationwide. Every year, the Conservancy runs an Open Days program, allowing you to visit several outstanding gardens in one area on a given day. In 2015, 330 private gardens in 22 states participated in the Open Days Program. Since the garden owners are often hosts during the tour, you can learn about their plants and techniques.

Connecticut's Historic Gardens
cthistoricgardens.org

For the past 13 years, this group of 15 historic gardens has organized Connecticut's Historic Gardens Day, with each member site hosting a special event.

Garden State Gardens
gardenstategardens.org

Garden State Gardens is a consortium of New Jersey's public gardens formed to increase the public's awareness of and appreciation for the beauty and horticultural, educational, artistic and historic value of New Jersey's public gardens.

Greater Philadelphia Gardens
americasgardencapital.org

Greater Philadelphia Gardens is a consortium of more than 30 public gardens, arboreta, and historic landscapes, all located within 30 miles of Philadelphia.

Historic New England
historicnewengland.org

Historic New England is the oldest and largest regional heritage organization in the nation. The site preserves and maintains 36 properties spanning 5 states, as well as vast collections, publications, exhibitions, and archives that document more than 400 years of life in New England.

Hudson River Valley Heritage Area
hudsonrivervalley.com

Through a partnership with the National Park Service, this organization preserves and celebrates the cultural and natural resources of the Hudson River Valley.

The Trustees of Reservations
thetrustees.org

For more than 100 years, The Trustees have protected and preserved special places in Massachusetts, including historic mansions and their gardens.

National Trust for Historic Preservation
savingplaces.org

The National Trust for Historic Preservation protects significant places representing our diverse cultural experience by taking direct action and inspiring broad public support.

HORTICULTURAL SOCIETIES

Massachusetts Horticultural Society
masshort.org

Connecticut Horticultural Society
cthort.org

Pennsylvania Horticultural Society
phsonline.org

Rhode Island Horticultural Society
rihorticulturalsociety.org

New Jersey State Horticultural Society
njshs.org

Tower Hill Botanic Garden
towerhillbg.org

GARDEN CLUB FEDERATIONS

Garden Club Federation of Massachusetts
gcfm.org

Landscape Design Council of Mass.
ldcma.org

Garden Club Federation of Pennsylvania
pagardenclubs.org

Garden Club of New Jersey
gardenclubofnewjersey.com

Federated Garden Clubs of Connecticut
ctgardenclubs.org

Federated Garden Clubs of New York State
fgcnys.com

Federated Garden Clubs of Vermont
vermontfgcv.com

New Hampshire Federation of Garden Clubs
nhfgc.org

Rhode Island Federation of Garden Clubs
rigardenclubs.org

Resources

Gardens of the Garden State
Nancy Berner and Susan Lowry

Gardens of the Hudson Valley
Nancy Berner and Susan Lowry

*The Art of Gardening: Design Inspiration and
Innovative Planting Techniques from Chanticleer*
R. William Thomas

Longwood Gardens: 100 Years of Garden Splendor
Colvin Randall

Rescuing Eden: Preserving America's Historic Gardens
Caroline Seebohm

Beatrix Farrand: Private Gardens, Public Landscapes
Judith B. Tankard

Great Gardens of America
Tim Richardson

The New York Botanical Garden
Gregory Long & Anne Shellin, editor

*The Artist's Garden: American Impressionism and the
Garden Movement*
Edited by Anna O'Marley

Great Gardens of the Berkshires
Virginia Small

New England's Historic Homes & Gardens
Kim Knox Beckius

The Brother Gardeners
Andrea Wulf

An Affair with a House
Bunny Williams

A Way to Garden
Margaret Roach

Photo credits

All photography by Jana Milbocker except for the
following:

Joan Butler: 10, 44 top, 61, 91 top and bottom left, 111 bottom left, 224, 225 top, 226 top and bottom right, 242 top

Keri Ferland: 26 left, 27 top, 30, 31 middle and bottom left

Susan Mitrano: 55 bottom, 217 bottom

Susan Gordon: 123 middle

Eileen Jobson: 176, 177

Wyck House: 234, 235 top and left

Alison Shaw: 50

Polly Hill Arboretum: 51

Weston Nurseries: 86

Roseland Cottage: 128

Postman: 137 aerial

PostMan 1107: 155 aerial

Alfred Atmore Pope Collection, Hill-Stead Museum, Farmington, CT. Photo by Anne Day.: 154 top

Hill-Stead Museum, Farmington, CT: 154 Theodate Pope, 155 top

New York Botanical Garden: 188 top, 189 top

Heritage Museums & Gardens: 55 middle

Order Form

The Garden Tourist

120 Destination Gardens and Nurseries in the Northeast

BY JANA MILBOCKER

EMAIL ORDERS: thegardentourist@gmail.com

WEBSITE ORDERS: EnchantedGardensDesign.com

TELEPHONE ORDERS: Call 508-494-8768. Have your credit card ready.

POSTAL ORDERS: Enchanted Gardens, PO Box 6433, Holliston, MA 01746

Name:

Address:

City: State: Zip Code:

Telephone:

Email:

Number of books: x $21.95	$	
Sales Tax (Please add 6.25% tax to orders shipped to Mass.)	$	
Shipping ($3.50 single book, $2 each additional, US only)	$	
Total	$	

Make check payable to **Enchanted Gardens**

Thank you for your order and happy touring!

Visit EnchantedGardensDesign.com for information on lectures and consulting.

Enchanted Gardens

PO Box 6433, Holliston, MA 01746

enchantedgardensdesign.com

thegardentourist@gmail.com

508-494-8768